I0877790

ROMAN EMPERORS AND THEIR ILLNESSES

List of Plates

Contents

Acknowledgments

In developing this book, I am indebted to numerous people. However, I should like to express my particular thanks to Professor Vivian Nutton, Professor David Wardle, Professor David Langslow, Dr Marcel van Ackeren, Professor Laurence Totelin, Professor Axel Karenberg, Professor Karl-Heinz Leven, Dr Osamu Muramoto, Dr Piers Mitchell and David Brear; in addition to fantastic colleagues at Oxford (Professors David Mant and Robert Arnott) and Durham (Professors Holger Maehle, Alan Broadbent and Thorsten Fögen).

I am also very grateful to Heather Williams and Carol Trow at *Pen & Sword Books* for their brilliant advice, guidance and encouragement in bringing this second project to fruition.

But, above all, I must express my enormous gratitude to my wife Ailie for her constant support and patience over many, many years!

Preface

Navigating the interface between ancient and modern healthcare is extremely tricky. Linked to the Hippocratic writings it is possible to find common ground in relation to ethical principles such as beneficence and non-maleficence. However, beneath this broader consensus, there are numerous differences in, for example, the underlying theoretical frameworks, the therapies being offered, the training undertaken by healers and the regulatory frameworks.

As a general practitioner, Roman medicine often seems very distant from my day-to-day work but on occasion I might sense a point of contact, as in the various comments by the ancient medical authors Galen and Celsus on the doctor-patient relationship. But, especially in these situations, I need to tread carefully keeping in mind that, although I might study and learn about ancient medicine, I cannot, as a modern doctor, ever truly belong to the Roman past.

Interdisciplinary collaboration is essential to explore any aspect of ancient medicine and, in developing this book, I am very grateful for the two-year association I enjoyed with the University of Durham. I am particularly indebted to Holger Maehle for his invaluable insights into medical history; Alan Broadbent for his constructive philosophical comments and Thorsten Fögen for his phenomenal expertise and guidance in the technical aspects of ancient Greek and Latin.

Introduction

The ancient medical authors Pliny and Celsus both extolled the health benefits of seawater. Pliny in *Naturalis historia* compiled an extensive list of its medicinal uses, including treating ligament and joint pains, fevers, stomach problems, insect stings, scorpion bites, deafness, headache, breast swellings and chest disorders. The Roman Baths of Sliema carved out of solid rock on the Maltese coast are, according to local legend, where our ancient forbears immersed themselves in the salty waters seeking cures for a variety of ailments. One bath is rectangular with a curved end on the shore side in keeping with several Roman plunge pools I have visited over the years. However, in reality, the Sliema baths would never have been frequented by the ancient Romans as they were probably only cut during the nineteenth century, when Malta was part of the British Empire. At that time there were burgeoning interests in Roman Imperial power alongside the health benefits of sea water bathing.

The ancient medical past might be characterised as a foreign country, but it is also at risk of becoming an imaginary place. Misunderstandings of ancient medical literature by modern translators, reconstructing archaeological sites for tourists or re-interpreting artifacts based on today's sensibilities can easily lead to misinterpretations of the past. For example, the Latin words *phthisis, apoplexy* and *podagra* cannot simply be equated to modern-day tuberculosis, stroke or gout respectively. The archaeological identification of aqueducts, bathhouses and drainage systems probably says more about the aspirations of an ancient provincial town to appear 'Roman' than any particular concern for today's ideas about public health. In considering any aspect of ancient medicine it is also important to appreciate that our view of the past is constantly changing. The Victorian families involved in the commissioning of the Sliema baths might have been wedded to an idea of a glorious Roman Empire that they were seeking to mimic. Perhaps by domesticating an element of the Roman past they were nostalgic for, as they saw it, a more healthy and stress-free life.

Although many of today's doctors seem keen to exploit the past as a source for amusing anecdotes there is now much less interest in considering ancient writings or archaeological findings as tools to assist with improving modern-day healthcare or population wellbeing. This partially arises from a Whiggish perspective, where the thinking, medicine or science of an earlier time is considered inherently inferior to that of the present and the past is best portrayed as a series of events leading to a better future. The underlying assumption is that things only change by getting better and this progress has brought us to where we are today. Linked to this is a Presentist view that we can simply apply modern ideas and concepts to the health and healthcare of the distant past.

In *Greco-Roman Medicine and What It Can Teach Us Today*, I challenged the Whiggish approach to medical history by identifying topics distilled from the literature and archaeology of our Greco-Roman past that have the potential to impact positively on modern-day healthcare, population wellbeing or scientific knowledge. This included prevention and the preservation of health, Stoicism, healing sanctuaries and the identification of new medicines. This book examines the illnesses of the Roman emperors as I have become increasingly uncomfortable with the Presentist approach to diagnosing the diseases of historical figures. The socio-cultural and historical contexts are frequently sidelined in favour of concentrating solely on ancient reports of symptoms and signs. Such an approach encourages uncontrolled, inappropriate and unwarranted speculation.

This work commences by outlining the questions and issues to be considered in seeking to diagnose illnesses in historical figures. A detailed focus on Emperor Augustus next serves as an opportunity to reconstruct an ancient health profile and to evaluate the available evidence prior to generating any diagnostic conjectures. The remainder of the book then offers fresh insights into the health of the emperors Tiberius, Caligula, Claudius, Nero, Marcus Aurelius and Lucius Verus. Covering seven different men enables consideration to be given to a wide range of purported mental and physical problems in addition to seeking to augment historical understanding.

CHAPTER 1

Diagnosing the Past

Retrospective diagnosis is the practice of identifying an illness after the death of a patient using modern knowledge, disease classifications and methods. It is also important to distinguish between retrospective diagnoses that are made shortly after the death of an individual using current pathology and laboratory techniques and retrospective diagnoses of historical figures and/or historical diseases using archaeological materials, documents and artifacts.

Analysing the diseases and deaths of long-dead rulers, artists and musicians to understand more about their lives is often seen as a fascinating line of enquiry. For example, in relation to the first seventeen Roman emperors, the suggested causes of death are detailed in the table below:

Causes of death for the first seventeen Roman emperors

Emperor	Years of rule	Age at death	Suggested cause(s) of death (in modern terms)
Augustus	41	75	Gastroenteritis (? poisoned)
Tiberius	22	77	Heart attack (? murdered)
Caligula	4	28	Murder
Claudius	14	63	Heart attack or stroke (? poisoned)
Nero	14	30	Suicide
Galba	7 months	70	Murder

Emperor	**Years of rule**	**Age at death**	**Suggested cause(s) of death (in modern terms)**
Otho	3 months	36	Suicide
Vitellius	8 months	54	Murder
Vespasian	10	69	Gastroenteritis
Titus	2	41	Malaria
Domitian	15	44	Murder
Nerva	2	67	Malaria
Trajan	19	63	Stroke (? poisoned)
Hadrian	21	62	Heart failure. Hereditary haemorrhagic telangiectasia
Antoninus Pius	23	74	Food poisoning
Marcus Aurelius	19	58	Exhaustion, suicide (? smallpox)
Lucius Verus	8	38	Stroke (? poisoned)

A few of the later Roman emperors are also said to have died naturally from infectious diseases (e.g. Claudius Gothicus), chronic health problems (e.g. Septimius Severus and Constantius I) or stroke (e.g. Valentinian I). In addition, some more novel suggestions have been proposed such as carbon monoxide poisoning (Jovian) or being struck by lightning (Carus).

However, some medical historians, including Andrew Cunningham, have raised concerns about the rigour of the approaches being adopted to diagnose past illnesses and the veracity of any outputs. Deficiencies have been highlighted in the formulation of research questions; the approaches to data acquisition; and the assessment of the validity of any information identified. It is also important to confront three broad questions: is it justifiable to use modern medical knowledge to generate retrospective diagnoses of historical figures; if an historical figure had a real disease (in modern terms), is it possible to determine what disease they had; and are there ethical and professional issues that need to be addressed in formulating retrospective diagnoses of historical figures?

To properly understand a Roman emperor's illness(es) and/or cause of death there are five fundamental issues to consider:

1. The Nature of Retrospective Diagnosis

The earlier definition of retrospective diagnosis implies that it is confined to the practice of identifying an illness. But, perhaps, a more clinically relevant characterisation of diagnosis is as a process as opposed to a tool for disease classification.

- Modern diagnosis starts when a patient experiences a health problem.
- Modern diagnosis is a step-by-step process, incorporating cycles of information gathering, interpretation and hypothesis generation.
- Most modern diagnosis is probabilistic, incrementally reducing uncertainty as further clinical data is gathered. Identifying the most likely diagnosis will clearly result in better overall care.

I would suggest that the retrospective diagnosis of Roman emperors should also be viewed as an iterative process, in which information is carefully assembled and assessed. It is also probabilistic in that, although we can never be totally confident about the health problems affecting a Roman emperor, we ought to strive to increase the certainty as to the presence or absence of health problems.

Unlike modern diagnosis, retrospective diagnosis is not about delivering better patient care, but it should still focus on outputs such as considering the potential influence of putative diseases on an individual's activities or behaviours, and examining what it was like to live with certain diseases in Ancient Rome (albeit with the caveat that most emperors will have been at the elite end of the care spectrum).

Identifying and addressing retrospective misdiagnoses might also serve to adjust the historical record and our modern perceptions about some of the Roman emperors.

2. The Importance of Context

In 1913 the scientist and historian Charles Singer came across the twelfth century illuminated *Scrivias* manuscript that described the religious visions (including thirty-five miniature illustrations) experienced by Abbess Hildegard of Bingen. A translation of part of the accompanying text described 'a clouding over of my eyes, and I was so pressed down by the weight of my body that I could not raise myself'.[1] Singer concluded that the Abbess had been experiencing visual auras consistent with migraine, a clinical picture that had first been described in the medical literature just a few years previously. But in making this retrospective diagnosis he ignored the medieval context; specifically, Hildegard's own medical expertise in addition to her interpretation of the illnesses as divine punishment. This highlights the risk that retrospective diagnosticians consider historical and religious records in the same way as they might modern scientific or clinical evidence, ascribing pathology to behaviours that require none. Despite many reservations being raised about Singer's analysis and conclusions, the idea that Hildegard had migraine has now become firmly entrenched in the popular medical literature. For example, in his book *Migraine,* Oliver Sacks wrote 'a careful consideration of these accounts and figures leaves no doubt concerning their nature: they are undisputedly migrainous.'[2]

According to the Christian author Lucius Lactantius (c240–320), the Roman Emperor Galerius came to a horrible end. He was said to have died of extensive chronic ulceration of the abdomen and genitals which lasted about a year and, eventually, 'his bowels came out, and his whole seat putrefied…worms were generated in his body. The stench was so foul as to pervade not only the palace, but even the whole city…and his body, with intolerable anguish, was dissolved into one mass of corruption.' After a careful analysis of the description of Galerius' terminal symptoms by several modern physicians, it was concluded that his death was due to Fournier's gangrene. This is a rare, life-threatening infection that rapidly destroys flesh in the genital and lower abdominal areas. However, in making such a retrospective diagnosis it is important to consider Lactantius' final comment too. 'At length overcome by calamities, he was obliged to acknowledge God, and he cried aloud in the intervals of raging pain, that he would re-edify the Church which he had demolished and make atonement for his misdeeds.' Lactantius' book – tellingly entitled *De mortibus persecutorum* (On the Deaths of the Persecutors) – also detailed the troubled ends of the Emperors Diocletian and Licinius. Perhaps there is a need to consider if there might have been some significant embellishment in the descriptions of the symptoms and the deaths of all three emperors, emphasising the severe consequences for those who persecute Christians!

Several authors have highlighted contextual challenges linked to temporal changes in medical knowledge/theories, technology, sanitation, nutrition, environment, economics, religion and working conditions. It is even suggested that any attempt at the retrospective diagnosis of historical figures should mandate researchers to act and think in accordance with the medical knowledge, attitudes and practices in addition to the social norms (e.g. political, religious, cultural) of the past in coming to any decisions. If the dates of the various retrospective diagnoses of Chopin are arranged in chronological order, these correlate with contemporary research in clinical medicine from tuberculosis (1899), through allergic conditions (1961) to alpha-1-antitrypsin deficiency (1994).[3] There is little doubt that the writer Jonathan Swift exhibited cognitive symptoms, memory changes and alterations in his personality. However, the various retrospective diagnoses suggested to account for Swift's clinical condition probably say more about the varying attitudes regarding the significance of certain symptoms for neurological and psychiatric diagnoses over the last 300 years.[4]

One approach to help to address such contextual concerns might be to compare the clinical picture of the historical figure with other individuals from the same socio-cultural milieu. Understanding contemporary medical practices and writings in addition to the historical context are essential elements in generating any retrospective diagnosis.

3. The Problem of Language

A particular challenge in unravelling the illnesses of the Roman emperors is correctly interpreting the ancient Latin or Greek describing a possible medical condition. Therefore, on occasions, some specific Greek or Latin medical terms need to be particularly carefully dissected.

The Latin word *phthisis* (Ancient Greek: φθίσις), for example, which many translators equate to diseases such as consumption (in the nineteenth century) or tuberculosis (in the twentieth century) originally had a much broader meaning in Ancient Greece as a state of 'passing away'. It could be applied to any kind of disappearance such as the setting of the sun, the waning of the moon or the shrinking of the pupil of the eye. Herodotus first used the term medically to describe an accident affecting the general Pharnuches in 481BC:

> As they set forth from Sardis, an unwelcome mishap befell him: a dog ran under the feet of the horse he was riding, and the horse was taken by surprise and frightened, so it reared up and threw Pharnuches; after his fall he vomited blood and began to waste away [*phthisin*].

It has been suggested that Pharnuches had developed pulmonary tuberculosis, but this diagnosis is far too specific given the context and the information provided by Herodotus. Six hundred years later, by the time of the physician Galen, '*phthisis*' was characterised as 'ulceration of the lung or chest or throat; it brings on coughing and light fevers, along with wasting of the body' but, again, this description potentially encompasses a wide range of modern-day medical conditions.

Several members of the Roman elite – including the Emperors Vespasian and Septimius Severus alongside Augustus' right-hand man Marcus Agrippa – are said to have suffered from gout. The Greek word that is generally translated as gout is 'ποδάγρα' (Latin: '*podagra*') but the literal meaning is 'foot trap', emphasising the sudden pain often experienced in the metatarsophalangeal joint of the great toe. The term 'gout', first used to describe podagra by Randolphus of Bocking (1197–1258), is actually derived from the Latin word '*gutta*' (drop), referring to the prevailing medieval belief that an excess of one of the four humours would, under certain circumstances, drop or flow into a joint, causing pain and inflammation. A modern doctor confronted with a patient describing a sudden onset of pain within the great toe would consider gout but also alternative diagnoses such as septic/inflammatory arthritis, cellulitis, pseudogout in addition to a stress/march fracture. Vespasian, Septimius Severus and Marcus Agrippa might have suffered from a condition akin to our modern gout (and there is also skeletal evidence for gout in ancient Rome) but, after a life involving arduous campaigning, they could have easily developed stress/march fractures too.

The Emperor Septimius Severus' wife, Julia Domna, has been retrospectively diagnosed with modern-day breast cancer based on the following extract from Cassius Dio:

> One might say she was already in a dying condition by reason of the cancer (καρκίνος) of the breast that she had had for a very long time; it had, however, been quiescent until, on the occasion referred to, she had inflamed it by the blow with which she had smitten her breast on hearing of her son's death.

The ancient Greek word 'καρκίνος' literally means 'crab', perhaps based on a resemblance between the stretched veins over a swelling and the shape of a crab. The physician Galen mentioned 'καρκίνος' half a dozen times but made no categorical distinction between malignant and benign tumours. Today conditions such as bacterial mastitis, breast abscesses, fat necrosis and benign breast tumours can also cause swelling and distortion in the breast tissue that can be extremely difficult to distinguish from a breast cancer. Therefore, although Julia Domna might well have suffered from a breast disease, it is not appropriate to suggest anything more specific such as a cancer.

4. The Concept of Disease

Disease is defined as any harmful deviation from the normal structural or functional state of an organism, generally associated with certain symptoms and signs and differing in nature from physical injury. Modern disease classification can be traced to the work of Thomas Sydenham in the seventeenth century. He sought to describe and categorise diseases such that, for example, 'the symptoms observed by Socrates in his illness may generally be applied to any other person afflicted with the same disease, in the same manner as the general marks of plants justly run through the same plants of every kind.' Nowadays diseases can be classified in a variety of ways including cause(s) (aetiology), disease processes, symptoms or the organ systems involved. Those in favour of the aetiological stance argue that diseases are best understood in terms of causes. For example, infection with the bacterium Mycobacterium tuberculosis is always necessary for tuberculosis to develop.

One of the challenges of labelling an individual with a disease is that it is first necessary to understand their normal condition; a sharp demarcation between disease and health is not always apparent. Consequently, in many circumstances (especially when there is no obvious single cause as in most psychiatric diseases) what constitutes a disease becomes socially framed. To Charles Rosenberg 'many physicians and laypersons have chosen to label certain behaviours as disease even when a somatic basis remains unclear, and possibly non-existent – one can cite the instances of alcoholism, homosexuality and hyperactivity.'[5] The eventual inclusion of post-traumatic stress disorder into the *Diagnostic and Statistical Manual of Mental Disorders* serves as a good example of how a modern disease classification system required adjustment to accommodate 'a disease that was present but previously unseen' for social reasons.

Terms related to disease such as illness and sickness are often used quite loosely too. Illness is a person's subjective experience of poor health (including situations where no disease can be identified) and sickness is the role negotiated with society. Sickness incorporates considerations of how a disease might be viewed by society and the way an individual reacts to a particular diagnosis. Linked to the impacts (or potential impacts) of being labelled with a specific disease such as epilepsy, some modern patients might be unwilling to accept a specific, assigned sick role. The metaphors used by a society for certain diseases may also help to explain something about the actions of an historical figure (including, perhaps, feigning certain illnesses or denying others).

In generating retrospective diagnoses of historical figures, Cunningham has argued that it is incorrect to assume the continuous identity of past diseases with modern diseases for socio-cultural reasons. He further suggested that researchers should focus their attention on 'how diagnosis happens' as 'the identity of any disease is made up of a compound of elements, of which the biological or medical is only one, and sometimes the least important one'. To Cunningham, diagnosis occurs when, for example, an individual within the same sociocultural context as a recently deceased patient says that the death was due to X, Y or Z. According to Vivian Nutton, a particular challenge in relation to Roman medicine is that 'ancient perceptions and descriptions of diseases and the ways they are classified are frequently impossible to correlate with diseases reported in a modern medical textbook'. For example, in today's medicine, fever is a symptom and yet to Roman medical writers such as Celsus and Galen it was a disease.

Cunningham's stance links to the broader philosophical debate between naturalists and normativists concerning the definitions of health and disease. In the diagnosis of specific diseases, naturalists will argue that these can be defined – at least in part – in value-free terms based on biological function, whereas normativists will maintain that they are inherently value-laden concepts. But, in generating retrospective diagnoses it does not seem unreasonable to assume that many disease entities existed before their clinical description and classification in modern terms. Therefore, I would argue that the diagnosis of a communicable disease caused by a single type of organism, with a high level of infectivity and significant adverse health impacts, might be considered more objective and value-free than would be the case for a multifactorial psychological condition such as anxiety or a neurological problem such as migraine. In relation to Emperor Antoninus Pius, for example, who died in 161 aged 74, it was reported in the *Scriptores Historiae Augustae* (*SHA*), that 'after he had eaten too much Alpine cheese [*Alpinum caseum*] at dinner, he vomited during the night and contracted a fever the next day. On the third day, when he saw that he was becoming worse, he entrusted the republic and his daughter to Marcus Aurelius'. In modern terms it appears likely that the elderly Antoninus succumbed to the effects of severe food poisoning (possibly related to the bacterium Staphylococcus aureus) resulting from cheese consumption rather than anything more sinister. Roman cheese was made from raw milk and we now know that such unpasteurised cheeses can harbour a variety of pathogenic bacteria including Salmonella, Escherichia coli, Campylobacter and Staphylococcus aureus. There is also robust genomic evidence that various species of staphylococcus were widespread in the contemporary local environment.

But, even if the retrospective diagnosis of certain infectious diseases can be argued to be less dependent on the sociocultural context (i.e. education, beliefs, values, attitudes, and religion), there might have been temporal changes in the biology of the infecting organism and public health factors (e.g. sanitation, nutrition, environment, communications and immigration). Although human physiology, anatomy and genetics have changed little over recent millennia, this is not the case for bacteria and viruses. The term 'pathomorphosis' has also been coined to emphasise that the relations between microbes and men are subject to evolution including the baseline level of immunity in the population.

A different spectrum of diseases might have existed in the past too with the exclusion or the inclusion of certain conditions. Grmek (1989) uses the term 'pathocoenosis' to characterise the ensemble of pathological states present in a specific population at a given moment in time. In relation to Ancient Rome, Galen wrote 'this populous city, where daily ten thousand people can be discovered suffering from jaundice, and ten thousand from dropsy'.

Diseases we recognise today might also have been described through different illness experiences previously. For example, the distinct Greco-Roman theories as to how the body worked could have influenced how health problems were described by ancient patients, doctors and medical writers. Medical terms and categorisations might have altered their meaning too. Prior to the discovery of specific *Rickettsia* bacteria in the early twentieth century, the term 'typhus' was applied to a range of conditions later categorised as plague, yellow fever, typhoid fever as well as epidemic and murine typhus. Similarly, the historical term 'consumption' is often simply equated with tuberculosis, but contemporary tuberculosis is caused by the bacterium Mycobacterium tuberculosis whereas historical tuberculosis (consumption) might have included the conditions caused by Mycobacterium bovis too.

5. The Information Sources

There are three main types of information that might be used to generate retrospective diagnoses of historical figures: paleopathology; contemporary representations on coins, paintings, book illustrations and sculptures; plus, various ancient documents (including inscriptions) and literature.

Palaeopathology is the study of diseases and injuries through the analysis of mummified tissue, skeletal remains and coprolites (preserved faeces). Alongside the macroscopic and microscopic examination of bones for disease changes, additional information might be derived from imaging (e.g. computed tomography scanning) and molecular biology (e.g. DNA analyses). Such data might sometimes assist specifically, as in the case of the remains of Richard III found under a car park in Leicester, but more commonly furnish a picture of the diseases that were most prevalent at the time of a historical figure.

Representations of historical figures on coins, paintings, book illustrations and sculptures might be helpful in generating retrospective diagnoses. But in relation to the Roman emperors, it can be challenging to distinguish clinical data from any subtle political messaging or artistic stylisation. Also, although many Roman sculptures would have been painted highlighting features including skin colouration, such embellishments cannot now be clearly characterised. On occasions, the addition of cultural or religious symbolism can generate confusion if such information is misinterpreted as showing pathological features.

Some contemporary coins of the Roman Emperor Maximinus Thrax portray him with heavy features, a pronounced forehead and a protruding jaw. This information accords with the descriptions of his physical appearance provided by both Herodian and the *SHA*. The former wrote that 'the emperor's appearance was frightening and his body was huge; not easily would any of the skilled Greek athletes or the best-trained warriors among the barbarians prove his equal' and, in the *SHA*, that 'he was of such size that men said he was six inches over eight feet in height; and his thumb was so huge that he used his wife's bracelet for a ring.' Some doctors have latched onto this information, suggesting that he was suffering from the modern disease acromegaly, due to the overproduction of growth hormone, but it is equally plausible that he was simply being represented as a powerful warrior. The *SHA* certainly commented that 'in his early youth he was a herdsman and the leader of a band of young men, a man who would waylay marauders and protect his own folk from forays.'

In his biographies of each Roman emperor, Suetonius included a description of body size and shape in addition to commenting on their complexion, hair, nose, eyes and mouth. At the time there was a particular interest in physiognomics, a view that a person's outward appearance could reveal their true character. For example, being of above average height and well-proportioned was associated with the Roman virtues of courage and a sense of duty and it is quite possible that this pseudoscience impacted on the various representations of the emperors. Undoubtedly, many Julio-Claudian busts are stylistically similar; Caligula's aligns with those of Tiberius and Augustus including, for example, the typical Julio-Claudian arrangement of the hair on the forehead.

Perhaps to distance himself from Nero, the Emperor Vespasian's images reverted to the more life-like representations common during the period of the Roman Republic. This more naturalistic tendency in portraiture perhaps increases the potential to spot diagnostically useful signs and several representations of Hadrian – including examples from museums in London, Athens, Madrid, Rome and Florence – exhibit a diagonal earlobe crease. Medically this feature is termed 'Frank's sign' and is supposedly associated with an increased risk of developing heart disease.

However, in general, most of the information used for the retrospective diagnoses of historical figures (including the Roman emperors) is derived from written sources. It is helpful to distinguish medical texts (written by physicians for their colleagues) from historiographic documents (e.g., chronicles, letters, speeches written by medical laymen which touch on medical subjects) and religious writings, including magic, dealing with health and disease. All these sources provide different types of 'data' and reminds us that such information should be considered within the relevant temporal and cultural context. Of the various sources it has been suggested that medical writings are more likely to be influenced by the various contemporary theoretical understandings and concepts. Leven cites the description provided by Anna concerning her father's symptoms (the Byzantine Emperor Alexius I Comnenus (1081-1118)): '[he perceived] a very heavy stone on his breast which made breathing difficult.'[6] But even in this situation, Anna went on to consider and explain her father's problems in terms of contemporary Hippocratic/Galenic medical theories. Also, there is a requirement to be careful in interpreting exactly what is meant by Anna's words and not to simply assume she meant a 'feeling of tightness in the chest' consistent with our modern angina. In addition, great caution always needs to be attached to translations and to be aware of possible copying errors in relation to the transmission of ancient documents.

In appraising data sources, it is important to be wary of bias, confounding, and the chance survival of selected items. In reporting a symptom, sign or health issue a Roman emperor or their ancient biographer might have sought to magnify, minimise or distort clinical information for socio-cultural reasons. Medical writers will also not necessarily share my views – as a modern doctor – as to what information is or isn't clinically or diagnostically relevant. All ancient authors might, on occasion, have adjusted their reporting according to how they – or their patron – felt about a particular emperor or, more generally, the Principate as opposed to the Republic. A confounder is a factor (e.g. culture, education, knowledge, malnutrition) that might influence both the retrospective diagnosis and, independently, the clinical data recorded in the historical records leading to a spurious association.

More broadly, it is essential to adopt a comprehensive and systematic approach to identifying all relevant sources as well as avoiding taking the incidental mention of a possible health condition out of the historical context as an 'isolated medical report'. Throughout this book the major ancient medical sources that have been enlisted to examine the illnesses of the Roman Emperors are Celsus (c.25BC–AD50) and Galen (129–216). The precise details of the general references vary considerably by emperor but the following constitute the major ancient general sources consulted: Tacitus (c.56–c.120), Suetonius (c.69–c.122) and Cassius Dio (c.165–c.235).

Tacitus is generally acknowledged as the premier historian of the Julio-Claudian period and his *Annales* – covering the Emperors Tiberius, Caligula, Claudius and Nero – was probably begun around 115. Although he was a good researcher and presented his facts about emperors honestly and with balance it is important to appreciate that he was opposed to the Principate as a constitutional form, admiring the senatorial system within the Republic instead.

Suetonius is considered a biographer rather than a historian with his *De vita Caesarum*, probably written around 120, covering all the emperors from Augustus to Domitian. In common with Tacitus, he consulted reliable sources and even reproduced extracts from the imperial correspondence. As his approach was more the thematic than chronological, he is a rich source of information on the emperors' personalities, appearances, health problems, habits and family backgrounds. His work is also a blend of historical information and anecdote covering both the private and public aspects of the emperors' lives (including relating juicy gossip). But in making use of Suetonius' works it is important to appreciate that he was interested in determining each emperor's character by balancing individual virtues and vices with Augustus serving as his exemplar. He often focused on cruelty versus clemency; liberality versus luxury/lust; generosity versus avarice; and civility versus pride in describing an emperor.

Cassius Dio produced his eighty-volume history (covering 1,400 years) during the first quarter of the third century. He was writing when the Principate was firmly established and, having also served a senator, it has been suggested that the way he reported on events during the first century is more accepting of the imperial system. Compared to both Tacitus and Suetonius he also exhibited hostility to some early emperors such as Nero. Cassius Dio has been characterised by some classicists as somewhat pedestrian and unreliable, simply assembling facts. However, over recent years his historical importance has been re-evaluated and, certainly in the context of this book, he is a rich and complementary source of medical information.

Generating Retrospective Diagnoses of the Roman Emperors

In appreciation of the three broad questions and the five fundamental issues highlighted within this chapter, the following approach to generating retrospective diagnoses of the Roman emperors is suggested:

Adopting a model

Modern clinical diagnosis can be sub-categorised by setting i.e. hospital-based and primary care-based. In generating retrospective diagnoses several characteristics of the primary care diagnostic model are relevant: the high likelihood of undifferentiated, confusing or vague disease presentations; the perceived importance of context; the frequent reliance on descriptive information alone; the levels of diagnostic precision and uncertainty as well as the approach to disease verification. To ensure that any retrospective diagnostic outputs are contextualised, entirely based on the available data sources and at an appropriate level of precision, having the primary care model in mind to guide the process can be invaluable.

Comparing modern-day and retrospective diagnosis

Characteristics	Modern hospital-based diagnosis	Modern primary care-based diagnosis	Retrospective diagnosis of the Roman emperors
Likelihood of undifferentiated, confusing or vague disease presentations (as opposed to standard 'textbook' descriptions of typical cases)	Medium	High	High
Perceived importance of context (including disease prevalence) in generating a diagnosis	Low	High	High
Reliance on descriptive information (oral/written) alone	Rare	Common	Very common
Level of diagnostic uncertainty	Low	Medium-high	High
Level of diagnostic precision	High	Medium-low	Low
Use of histopathology for disease verification	Common	Occasional	Rare

Formulating the question(s)

Retrospective diagnostic questions might include: did an individual have a disease (in modern or ancient terms); if an individual had a real disease, what type of disease did that have in modern terms; what effects might a particular disease have had on an individual's activities and behaviours; and what would it have been like to live with a particular disease in Ancient Rome?

In formulating question(s), it is particularly important to avoid setting retrospective diagnosis aside from other areas of historical enquiry. According to Osamu Muramoto,[7] 'a retrospective diagnosis should be evaluated as a theory which competes with other non-medical theories in a larger context of the humanities and social sciences.' Ideally, question setting should also involve multidisciplinary collaboration between, for example, clinicians, historians, archaeologists, paleopathologists and medical philosophers.

There are ethical issues that might apply to any historical individual being subject to a retrospective diagnosis, especially as they cannot give consent, speak for themselves, be examined or undergo further diagnostic testing. If the available data is insufficient, then careful consideration needs to be given as to the appropriateness of generating a retrospective diagnosis. Also, it seems unsatisfactory to suggest a precise diagnosis that, because it would require verification using modern-day technologies, can never be properly confirmed.

Acquiring and appraising data

Careful consideration needs to be given to comprehensively and systematically identifying potential ancient sources for possible health-relating presentations and outcomes alongside the general and medical contexts. This might entail examining unpublished or untranslated information too.

Information requirements (where possible) should include: medical history (symptoms, signs, past medical history, illnesses/treatments, behaviours, associations, lifestyle and changes over time); aetiological and influencing factors (predisposing factors, precipitating factors, perpetuating factors and protective factors); and contextual information (historical, social, cultural, political, educational, medical/health-related, technological, religious, economic, environmental).

Information appraisal should consider the effects of chance, bias, and confounding.

Generating outputs

Linked to the retrospective diagnostic question(s) there will be two broad categories of outputs: diagnostic and historical. Careful consideration will need to be given to any uncertainties in the evidence and the appropriate level of diagnostic precision too.

Within modern primary care settings, disease classification continues to present a challenge due to issues such as the broad and unrefined nature of the problems encountered. The various iterations of the *International Classification of Disease* struggle to accommodate many of the health concerns addressed by general practitioners. Partially because of this, the decisions made by primary care clinicians are dissimilar from those made by specialists, with more emphasis on dichotomous categories. Considering the likely information available to the retrospective diagnostician – in addition to the context – it is suggested that a similar approach should be adopted with the use of broad categorisations. Different levels of diagnostic uncertainty will need to be accommodated by retrospective diagnosticians compared to modern diagnosticians, given the amount of data available from historical sources. Modern primary care clinicians also rely more heavily on oral descriptive information than their specialist colleagues and accommodate a higher level of diagnostic uncertainly. Moreover, much of the 'diagnostic verification' within primary care depends on temporal changes or responses to treatment rather than the use of histopathology. Therefore, in appreciation of the uncertain and imprecise nature of retrospective diagnoses (and the suggested analogies with modern-day primary care diagnosis) the following categories are suggested as a mechanism to guide retrospective diagnostic outputs:

Suggested categories for retrospective diagnostic conjectures

Levels of retrospective diagnostic certainty	Categorisation of an emperor's condition
Low	A disease confirmed or rejected based on ancient terminology and/or modern terminology
Medium	Dichotomous disease classification based on modern terminology (e.g. communicable versus non-communicable; physical versus psychological)
High	Analogy to a modern disease

On occasions it might be possible to comment that, for example, the 'condition had some features in common with modern-day malaria' or 'malaria is the most likely modern-day equivalent' (high certainty). However, more frequent outcomes will be 'the condition cannot be linked with any confidence to any specific modern-day disease but may represent an infectious disease' or 'the condition cannot be linked with any confidence to any category of modern-day diseases' (low-medium certainty). Whenever possible, an attempt should also be made to consider any diagnostic conjectures within the ancient context with a view to augmenting historical understanding.

CHAPTER 2

Health and Healers

Health

The average life expectancy at birth in Ancient Rome was estimated to lie between 22 and 25 years. However, this figure is skewed by the effects of high infant and childhood mortality rates so, if these are factored out, it is suggested that those who survived to their mid-teens might then be expected to live to around 48 to 54 years. Such data highlights the likely impact of acute infectious diseases including typhoid, tuberculosis, malaria and the various infectious diarrhoeal conditions within the Roman population.

Based on information derived from early Christian epitaphs (fourth and fifth centuries) together with records inscribed on cinerary urns from the first century BC, there is specific evidence of increased death rates affecting all age groups between August and October in Ancient Rome. During the winter months, individuals over the age of 50 exhibited a second peak of mortality too. From a modern-day perspective, the increased death rate amongst older individuals between November and January is unsurprising and was probably associated with an increased prevalence of infectious respiratory diseases during the cooler months. However, the summer mortality peak across all ages is more distinctive and might be linked to seasonal malaria compounded by immigration of young adults from healthier – malaria-free – areas. The episodic flooding of Rome by the River Tiber may also have been associated with outbreaks of infectious diseases including malaria.

Alongside historical, epigraphic and skeletal evidence there is now a growing body of archaeogenetic findings confirming the existence of various forms of malaria during the Roman period. *Plasmodium falciparum* malaria mitochondrial DNA fragments have been identified within the molars of two adults buried in southern Italy during the first to second century. There is also indirect evidence for the spread of malaria linked to the discovery of human genetic mutations (i.e. β-thalassaemia and glucose-6-phosphate dehydrogenase deficiency) in ancient Mediterranean populations.

It seems likely that the various Roman emperors were subject to much the same conditions as the remainder of the population. Even if some enjoyed a better diet than many of their subjects, they would have been exposed to a similar – or even worse – burden of infectious diseases within overcrowded environments such as the city of Rome or army camps. As Walter Scheidel points out 'for all their wealth and power, Roman emperors could not hope to live significantly longer than their subjects even if they managed to steer clear of daggers, poison and the battlefield.'[8] The Emperors Augustus and Vespasian probably succumbed to gastroenteritis, and it has been suggested that the Emperor Titus and the Emperor Nerva were affected by malaria.

In ancient battles around a quarter of wounded soldiers would die within ten days and nearly two-thirds of these deaths were due to blood loss with the remainder being caused by sepsis, gangrene and tetanus. In an analysis of mortality in the Roman Republican Army it is estimated that the average fatality rates in battles ranged from 4 to 16 per cent, with more deaths being linked to defeats. The death rate amongst the Roman troops from other causes, such as infectious diseases, was around 1.9 to 2.6 per cent per annum.

Healers

Some Roman patients might have had access to a physician, but many would have turned to a variety of other individuals to help with their health problems such as root cutters, gymnastic trainers, dream interpreters, eunuchs, boxers, grooms, pharmacists, midwives and priests. Pharmacists (including those who made – *unguentaria* – or sold – *seplasiarii* – ointments) were widespread across the Empire and probably occupied an important place in supplying patients with remedies. A limestone stela from Rome shows a female pharmacist with a book resting on her knee and surrounded by numerous barrels and circular objects. Behind her are two colleagues; one is shown adding materials to a vat and the other is stirring the mixture.

However, in considering the medical services available to the Romans it is important to be particularly careful in applying our modern labels. For example, Pliny wrote to the Emperor Trajan about a healer who had saved his life:

> Last year, Sir, when I was in serious ill-health and was in some danger of my life I called in an *iatralipten*, and I can only adequately repay him for the pains and interest he took in my case if you are kind enough to help me. Let me, therefore, entreat you to bestow on him the Roman citizenship.

But it is unclear whether Pliny's *iatralipten* was a physical therapist, ointment doctor or masseur.

The idea of a personal professional physician was anathema to many Romans. It was at odds with their values of self-sufficiency and looking after your own. On some Roman farms the head of the household enjoyed the role of chief healer with responsibility for the health of his family and any estate workers. The Roman agriculturist and farmer Varo wrote, 'There are two divisions....in the treatment of human beings: in the one case the physician should be called in, while in the other even an attentive herdsman is competent to give the treatment.' One of the Vindolanda writing tablets demonstrates that the women of military families were sometimes expected to deal with the day-to-day health problems that arose in their households and kept a selection of medicines to hand for this purpose. In letter 294, Paterna wrote to Lepidina: 'I shall supply you with two remedies', one of which was for fever.

Many aspects of Roman culture and society were strongly influenced by the Greeks and their impact on Roman medicine was particularly dominant. The earliest recorded reference to Rome's interaction with Greek medicine occurred in 293BC when, according to the Roman historian Livy, the god Aesculapius arrived in Rome in the form of a snake. Rome had experienced three consecutive years of plague and, after consulting the Sibylline Books, an embassy was dispatched to Greece seeking divine medical assistance. Around seventy years later, the Greek physician Archagathus migrated to Rome from the Peloponnese and was asked to stay. According to Pliny the Elder:

> …citizen rights were given him, and a surgery at the cross-way of Acilius was bought with public money for his own use. They say that he was a wound specialist, and that his arrival at first was wonderfully popular, but presently from his savage use of the knife and cautery he was nicknamed 'executioner' and his profession, with all physicians, became objects of loathing.

These comments by Pliny – together with those of others at the time – illustrate Roman distrust for the Greek influence on medicine. But, despite these initial forgivings, Greek physicians flocked into Rome encouraged, to some extent, by Julius Caesar's grants of citizenship and Augustus' tax exemptions for medical practitioners. The growing prosperity of the city would have increased the demand for medical services too. Soon the Romans were adopting many Greek healing practices in addition to assimilating their medical vocabulary into Latin.

Physicians

Emperors, governors and men of substance were often attended by personal physicians who would often travel with them. During one imperial progress, Apollinarus, physician to the Emperor Titus, even commented on a successful visit to the toilet in Herculaneum, by scratching on the wall the words: '*Apollinaris medicus Titi Imp; hic cacavit bene*'. The Emperor Septimius Severus, who is said to have suffered badly from gout, certainly had two doctors in attendance upon him during his Scottish campaign. On the return of the emperor to York, the physicians received instructions from his son, Caracalla, that they should hasten the death of Septimus Severus. Their refusal was disastrous for them, and it is possible that their remains are amongst the beheaded skeletons unearthed at York in 2005.

There is epigraphic evidence for the presence of physicians right across the Roman Empire. Moreover, numerous inscriptions from the west, including Britain, indicate that around two-thirds of doctors were Greek or of Greek descent. For example, two altars written in Greek and dedicated by doctors have been found in Chester and can be translated as:

> To the mighty Saviour Gods, I Hermogenes a doctor set up this altar.

> The doctor Antiochus honours the all-surpassing saviours of men among the immortals. Asclepius of the gentle hands, Hygeia and Panakeia.

The text on the altar by Antiochus is particularly poetic, perhaps an attempt to emphasise his educated status. But, whether either Hermogenes or Antiochus were legionary doctors, civilian doctors or perhaps personal physicians to senior officials remains uncertain. Intriguingly, Hadrian's personal physician was also called Hermogenes.

There were also a range of specialist physicians within Rome such as those treating eye problems (*ocularius*), ear disorders (*auricularius*) alongside those undertaking surgery. Across the Empire there is evidence of female doctors, such as Flavia Hedone (Nimes, France), Matilia Donata (Lyon, France), Julia Saturnina (Emerita, Spain) and Sarmanna (Gondorf, Germany). On one side of Julia Saturnina's tombstone is a relief depicting a baby perhaps indicating her interests in obstetrics or paediatrics.

One of the impacts of Greek medicine on the Roman world was the employment of public physicians by some communities. Galen reported that, in his day, many cities provided surgeries where doctors could tend the sick. From the distribution of doctors – as attested by inscriptions – across the southern Gallic province of Narbonensis, it is interesting to note that that most major towns boasted one or more physicians. There is one inscription from Arles, another from Vienne, two from Aix, three from Nimes and seven in Narbonne (the provincial capital).

However, despite all the evidence for physicians across the Empire, it is often unclear what led to an individual acquiring the title 'doctor'. There were no examinations, no diplomas, no degrees and no professional licensing procedures in the Roman world. A doctor was simply an individual who claimed the title and carried out treatment for some type of remuneration. Influential contacts, public positions and personal recommendations were much more important than qualifications in enabling doctors to retain patients as well as attracting new clients. Ulpian, the prominent second century Roman jurist, defined a physician as:

> one who promises a cure for any part of the body, or relief from pain, as, for example, an affection of the ear, a fistula, or a toothache; provided he does not employ incantations, imprecations, or exorcisms [to make use of the ordinary term applied to charlatans], for such things as this do not properly belong to the practice of medicine, although there are persons who commend such expedients, and affirm that they have been benefited by them.

The medical training undertaken to become a physician was also extremely variable in terms of time and content. Although some doctors worked as apprentices, there was no barrier to others simply setting themselves up in practice with a very minimal level of training. The physician Galen completed eleven years of study to build the foundations of his career, whereas Thessalus of Tralles claimed that the craft of medicine could be learned in six months by anyone. Starting at the age of 17, Galen worked as a medical student for two years in his native Pergamon before moving to Smyrna. This was followed by five years at Alexandria and a subsequent period of travel within Egypt, furthering his knowledge of pharmacology and anatomy. Alongside his medical training, he also studied philosophy and in his treatise *Quod optimus medicus sit quoque philosophus* (The Best Doctor is also a Philosopher). Galen emphasised the importance of doctors having a solid grounding in logic/reasoning, natural philosophy and ethics. Returning to Pergamon at the age of 28, Galen took up his first definitive position as doctor to the town's gladiators, providing him with a wealth of clinical and anatomical experience. Interestingly, according to an epitaph from Aix-en-Provence, the doctor Sextus Julius Felicissimus was attached to the amphitheatre there when he died at the age of 19. In addition to '*medicus*', Sextus was given the title of '*alumno*' which probably meant 'pupil'.

In certain cities, and in common with other craftsmen across the Roman world, some physicians formed themselves into medical colleges. At Metz, Sextus Publicius Decamanus was assigned the title '*collegii medicorum liberto*' (freedman of the college of doctors) on his tombstone. Other colleges certainly existed at Turin, Beneventum and Ephesus with evidence of medical contests between members.

During the early empire, it was not unusual for physicians to associate themselves with particular schools or sects and follow distinct approaches to caring for their patients. For example, on the memorial stone to the physician Marcus Apronius Eutropus from Vienne in Gaul he was termed '*medico Asclepiadio*' – a follower of Asclepiades of Bithynia. In addition, he was one of the select six Seviri Augustales, appointed for the year by the curia of their city, and chosen according to their wealth and status.

At the time of Galen, the two broad theoretical divisions were between the Empiricist and the Rationalist sects of physicians. However, Galen was probably not unique in basing his practice on both traditions according to the clinical circumstances. The Empiricists attached particular significance to carefully observing patients during the course of an illness, including the response to any treatments. They would also consider any previous findings made by themselves and others in similar situations. A treatment plan would then be selected by comparing the clinical features in their patient with those of conditions that it most resembled. Moreover, if a newly discovered or observed finding contradicted a previously held view, the old idea might be discarded or modified to accommodate the new circumstances.

Empiricist physicians acknowledged that it was useful to try to understand the obvious causes of diseases, but what mattered most was not what caused, but what cured a condition. Celsus, for example, argued that, in the past, effective treatments were discovered by people wise enough to notice that a specific approach was the best to treat a particular condition. He stated that 'the art of medicine was not a discovery following on reasoning, but after the discovery of the remedy, the reason for it was sought out.' To the Empiricist, it does not matter why a remedy works, only that it does work.

The Rationalists believed in the overriding importance of reason in formulating and adopting a theory concerning the structure and/or function of the body, and the nature of health and disease. They argued that every medical phenomenon and every disease had a cause (or causes) and that, while many of these were evident, others may be hidden from direct observation. It was then necessary to work out the most appropriate remedies for a disease or disorder linked to the underlying theoretical foundation. The Dogmatics might be considered a sub-division of the Rationalists in that their underlying theory was derived from the Hippocratic focus on the four humours, the four temperaments and the four basic qualities (see Chapter 3). The

Pneumatists also had overt Rationalist tendencies, but their emphasis was more about *pneuma* in understanding physiology and pathology.

Methodism was originally developed from the theories of Asclepiades of Bithynia by the Greek physician Themison. Despite loudly expressed reservations by Galen, it eventually became the dominant medical sect in the late Roman Empire. Methodists argued that all diseases shared some general and plainly visible characteristics, termed commonalities, and that a careful assessment of the patient would provide a good indication of these. According to Themison, there were three major categories of disease, based on 'stricture', 'looseness' or an 'intermediate', mixed, state. To the Methodists the primary focus of medicine was the individual patient, and phenomena as they were observed in the individual were the only realities of medicine.

Both the Greeks and the Romans were also concerned about the quality and the regulation of doctors. For example, Pliny the Elder wrote:

> The medical profession is the only one in which anybody professing to be a physician is at once trusted, although nowhere else is an untruth more dangerous. We pay however no attention to the danger, so great for each of us is the seductive sweetness of wishful thinking. Besides this, there is no law to punish criminal ignorance, no instance of retribution. Physicians acquire their knowledge from our dangers, making experiments at the cost of our lives. Only a physician can commit homicide with complete impunity.

On their part, physicians highlighted the importance of professional standards for physicians in addition to other healers. Galen proffered guidance on a doctor's clothes, nails, hair, cleanliness, odour in addition to the appropriate use of technical terms and correct grammar. He also provided patients with a list of questions they should put to a practitioner before engaging them. He particularly recommended that patients should observe practitioners at work and note how well (or badly) they treated the patient – including the accuracy of their prognoses.

Despite Roman physicians not being controlled by any formal institutions, there was a form of 'social regulation'. Although authority was in the hands of the healthcare providers, power remained in the hands of patients, with the freedom to choose from within a 'medical marketplace' in determining which therapeutic option to follow. They would also have had the opportunity to attend public displays of medical/anatomical skills, watch processions or medical competitions and gain an insight into a doctor's practice, clientele and reputation. A patient might even have observant friends clustering around their bed and the physician may arrive with an entourage or supporters and onlookers.

Military Medics

Inscriptions bearing the titles of *medicus alae, medicus castrensis/castrorum, medicus chirurgus, medicus clinicus, medicus cohortis, medicus duplicarius, medicus legionis* and *medicus ordinarius* have been found throughout the Roman Empire – in fact, there is currently evidence for medical personnel from sixty-seven Roman army sites. There continues to be considerable debate about the precise nature of the Roman army medical service in terms of personnel and organisation. Moreover, it seems likely that, as the Roman army developed and changed over the centuries, so too did the associated health care. It is generally agreed that military medics were appointed by the army, bestowed with a privileged legal position and sanctioned to attend to the soldiers. Their health-related responsibilities would have included ensuring that new recruits were physically fit; providing specialist treatment for battlefield injuries (e.g. wound care and missile extraction), general medical practice and, on some occasions, perhaps advising on healthy locations for the siting of permanent military bases.

In addition to the occasional Greek doctor, a range of medical assistance would have been available to the front-line soldiers. At the sharp end were the *capsarii*, the medical orderlies or dressers, the name being derived from the round bandage box (*capsa*) that they carried. These were probably ordinary soldiers concerned mainly with the first aid necessary during battle. Some may have been *immunes* with their medical work being deemed important enough to allow them to be excluded from regular duties. Furthermore, it seems likely that the *capsarii* were under the control of a doctor with the rank of centurion, the *medicus ordinarius*.

Divine healers

Religion was closely intertwined with all aspects of Roman life and, in appreciation of the limitations of terrestrial medicine, many individuals turned to the gods for help and guidance. Apollo was the original classical deity associated with medicine but, as time passed, Aesculapius (or Asclepius to the Greeks), the son of Apollo by Coronis, gradually became the god more clearly linked with health care. Aesculapius was born by Caesarean section and trained in medicine by the centaur Chiron. The young Aesculapius is also said to have been guarded by serpents and dogs – two animals that subsequently became associated with the Aesculapian creed. The offspring of Aesculapius included Acesis (Telesphorus), Hygeia (Salus) and Panacea.

The original Aesculapian sanctuaries were established at Epidaurus, Cos and Pergamum with the first Roman temple to Aesculapius being built on Tiber Island. Subsequently the cult spread widely across the Empire being popularised by physicians in addition to the Roman army. Some sites were even patronised by emperors and, as a result, saw their standing increase, leading to enrichment, revival and rebuilding. The Emperor Hadrian certainly visited Epidaurus and Pergamon and the Emperor Caracalla travelled around various sanctuaries seeking help from Apollo Grannus, Aesculapius and Serapis with 'many supplications and unwearying persistence. For even while abroad he sent to them prayers, sacrifices and votive offerings, and many couriers ran hither and thither every day carrying something of this kind; and he also went to them himself, hoping to prevail by appearing in person.'

However, although Aesculapius and his family were associated with health, it would be wrong to assume that healing was dissociated from the other ancient gods. Healing prayers or health-seeking offerings could be directed at any deity according to the individual's preference. There was also evidence for religious syncretism with the blending of Roman beliefs and approaches with local gods. For example, Eshmun at Sidon (Lebanon), Nodens at Lydney and Sulis Minerva at Bath (UK), Apollo Grannus at Grand (France), Lennus Mars at Trier (Germany), Serapis and Isis at Canopus (Egypt) and the merging of Aesculapius with the Thracian horseman at Glava Panega (Bulgaria). The Roman emperors themselves were sometimes associated with divine healing and, according to Suetonius:

> a man…who was blind, and another who was lame, came to [Vespasian] as he sat on the tribunal, begging for help for their disorders which Serapis had promised in a dream; for the god declared that Vespasian would restore the eyes, if he would spit upon them, and give strength to the leg, if he would deign to touch it with his heel…[Vespasian] was at last prevailed upon by his friends and tried both things in public before a large crowd; and with success.

The key facilities available at the major Aesculapian healing sites were a source of water – with wells, fountains and baths; temples; an *abaton* (dream room or dormitory), an area to exhibit votives and testimonials plus space for exercising, rituals, festivals, and processions. Some had libraries, theatres, banqueting halls, stadia, gymnasia and accommodation for visitors. Sleeping in an *abaton* (or, in some situations, elsewhere in the sanctuary) and undergoing a process of ritual incubation was a central element of the Aesculapian healing process.

During incubation, Aesculapius was said to appear in a dream-vision and either heal the individual directly or provide them with guidance about what was required to effect a cure. The process also involved priests and priestesses circulating among the sleepers with snakes and dogs, the curative dreams apparently being augmented by the touches of the priests or the licks of the animals. In some cases, individuals might have been given specific narcotic drugs such as opium too.

There is evidence that a variety of more traditional and holistic treatments were provided at many healing sites alongside communing with the appropriate deity or undertaking dream healing/incubation. Medical instruments have been found at Epidaurus and Corinth, and there is evidence for the prescription of medications at Epidaurus. Water was also an extremely important element of many healing sites and was drunk for its healing properties as well as being used for bathing, hydrotherapy and ritual cleansing. A variety of arts-type therapies were practised at many of the ancient healing sites involving music, visual arts, reading and writing (including producing and reciting poetry) in addition to drama. Arriving at Athens, Pausanius was particularly struck by the art works on display there, writing: 'The sanctuary of Aesculapius is worth seeing both for its paintings and for the statutes of the god and his children. In it there is a spring.' The sights of soaring marbled buildings, sculptures, paintings and images of healing gods at many sites must have been quite a dramatic – and uplifting – experience for many visitors.

Hearing music and singing would also have been common experiences. Flute-playing is mentioned in a play by Athenaios and the remains of musical instruments have been found at several locations. From Epidaurus and Pergamon there are reports of songs, hymns and even musical contests. The physician Asclepiades treated various mental disorders by music, soporifics (wine) and exercise and recommended that singing should be employed in the treatment of mania. Caelius Aurelianus wrote about the value of different varieties of piped music for symptoms of both anxiety and depression.

Many healing sites boasted splendid theatres and the example at Epidaurus still enjoys perfect acoustics allowing an audience of up to 14,000 to hear actors without electronic amplification. Such theatres would have been used for plays, celebrations of cures (including the singing of paeans), processions, festivals, games and choral performances. Viewing tragedies and comedies might also have formed part on an individual's treatment plan by putting their problems and worries into some sort of perspective.

CHAPTER 3

Roman Therapeutics

The Romans adopted a broad approach to therapeutics. The first century medical writer Celsus stated: 'medicine was divided into three parts, so that there was one which healed by regimen, another by drugs and a third manually. The Greeks named the first dietetics, the second pharmaceutics and the third surgery'. Scribonius Largus, a physician to the Emperor Claudius, emphasised the importance of balance in ensuring that drug treatments are used appropriately:

> freeing patients from pain and danger … we must condemn those who try to eliminate the use of drugs from medicine whereas we must support those who want to help the patient with all possible means…Indeed the physician helps patients by following certain steps. First, he tries to treat by allowing the appropriate food at the appropriate time; then if the patient does not respond to this treatment medicaments are given.

Several therapeutic options were available to the Roman patient: lifestyle modifications; pharmaceuticals; surgery; bathing and hydrotherapy; massage and rocking; cupping and phlebotomy.

Lifestyle modifications

The Romans and their doctors attached particular importance to following an appropriate lifestyle (termed 'regimen', 'hygiene' or 'dietetics') with a view to maintaining health.

Several Greek philosophers including Empedocles of Acragas developed the doctrine that all matter within the universe – including human bodies – was a mixture of four elemental substances (fire, air, water and earth) and four elemental qualities associated with them (hot, cold, wet and dry). Linked to this it was determined that the human body contained four humours – blood (hot and wet), yellow bile (hot and dry), black bile (cold and dry) and phlegm (cold and wet).

It was believed that the four humours needed to be in the correct amounts and strengths for a body to be healthy. The proper blending and balance of the four humours was known as '*eukrasia*'. Imbalance of humours – or '*dyskrasia*' – led to disease. In general, illness was about the excess or the lack of a specific humour or the exacerbation of one quality over another.

Importantly, humours were not considered to be present in equal quantities in everyone. Therefore, a physician wishing to re-balance an individual's humours had to consider a number of factors such as lifestyle, age and temperament in addition to the season.

The physician Galen proposed that lifestyle measures should be targeted at three groups: those who appear healthy already, those who are recovering from an illness and those who are in a state intermediate between heath and illness. The priority was to maintain the normal equilibrium of humours and qualities by recommending the correct kind and amount of, for example, food, drink, sleep, wakefulness and exercise. In *Ars medica* (The Art of Medicine) Galen outlined the key elements to consider in developing a healthy regimen as 'one from association with the ambient air, another from movement and rest of the whole body and its parts, a third from sleeping and waking, a fourth from those things taken in, a fifth from those things excreted or released, and a sixth from the affections of the soul'.

Ambient air

Pure air was particularly important to the Romans, and it was recommended to avoid air tainted by marshes, industrial processes, odours from drains or rotting remains. Galen was keenly aware of atmospheres that were 'stifling and foul, analogous to the air in houses that are shut up in which mould collects due to putrefaction and lack of ventilation. Such airs are harmful for all stages of life'. The first-century author Celsus advised his readers to reside in a house that is 'light and airy' and the lawyer Pliny emphasised the gentle breezes and the healthiness of the 'clear sky and the pure air' at his Tuscan villa. He also commented on the design of his Laurentine villa allowing 'the western breezes to enter and circulate' so that 'the atmosphere is never heavy with stale air'.

Smoke and fumes from the burning (or the partial burning) of carboniferous fuels for cooking or heating must have been a major problem for the Romans. It has been suggested that so many fires were lit across the Empire it caused a level of air pollution that cooled the European climate at the time. Seneca commented:

> No sooner had I left behind the oppressive atmosphere of the city and that reek of smoking cookers which pour out, along with the cloud of ashes, all the poisonous fumes they've accumulated in their interiors whenever they're started up, than I noticed the change in my condition at once.

In addition to affecting the levels and the balance of humours, air was relevant to two other important facets of ancient physiological theory – 'pneuma' and 'innate heat'. Pneuma was an ethereal substance derived, in part, from inspired air and circulated around the body enabling the key organs to function. Once it reached the rete mirabile at the base of the brain a psychic pneuma was produced which was responsible for consciousness, sensation and voluntary movement.

Originating in the heart, innate heat supported the vital functions of the human body. Over the course of a person's life it gradually lost strength, being eventually extinguished on death. According to Galen, it was 'preserved by the occurrence of moderate exercise, not only of the body but also of the mind'. Fresh air was seen as important in helping the innate heat to maintain its equilibrium, especially by cooling.

Based on a comparative study of ancient literature and the archaeological remains of the gardens at Pompeii, it has been proposed that the Roman idea of 'pure air' and health should be characterised broadly in terms of sensations and associations. Thus, the Romans might have recognised 'pure air' by the feel of a gentle breeze; the sounds of moving air, wildlife or water; light or sweet aromas as well as natural sights and colours especially blue, green and white.

Movement

According to Galen, 'for the preservation of health, exertions must come first, followed by food and drink, and next in order sleep, and, then sexual intercourse for those who engage in this.' He also made it clear than any movement could only be termed exercise or exertion if it brought about a change in breathing.

Celsus stated that 'useful exercises are reading aloud, drill, handball, running, walking; but this is not by any means most useful on the level, since walking up and downhill varies the movement of the body'. In addition to offering general advice on movement, Galen suggested specific exercises for different parts of the body writing:

> There are those that work out the loins more, or the arms, or the legs, and in other cases the whole spine, or the chest alone, or the lungs. In fact, walking and running are exercises specific for the legs, acrocheirism and shadow boxing are specific for the arms, bending forward and backward continuously for the loins.

He recommended taking very deep breaths or emitting very loud sounds to exercise the lungs. His views on sexual activity as exercise were that it was really designed for those in 'their prime', but subsequently he indicated that men at all ages should 'keep an eye on the use of sexual intercourse – whether it is harmless for them or harmful to those using it'.

Ancient healing sanctuaries, bathhouses and hospitals might have been designed to facilitate movement. The Roman architect Vitruvius was a particular advocate of the health benefits of exercise explaining that 'in walking the body is heated by motion, the air extracts the humours from the limbs'. At Hadrian's Villa in Tivoli there is a large open structure enclosing a garden with a central pool (*Poikile*). The north wall has a double portico with circular turning points at both ends incorporating an inscription stating the distance covered by walking alongside the wall. This ambulatory wall might even have been specifically orientated to ensure that one side provided shelter and warmth on winter walks with the other face offering shade during the hot summer months.

As with all lifestyle interventions Galen emphasised that one size does not fit all. 'Experience shows that some people are harmed and some are benefited by the same things…I know of some who immediately became sick, if they remain three days without exercise, and others who continue indefinitely without exercise and yet are healthy.' He went on to suggest that tailored exercise programmes might sometimes be required:

> There were some whom I prevented from exercising at all, even with those exercises that are suitable, wishing them to be satisfied with the activities of daily life only. Some, however, I ordered to set aside the majority of exercises, so as to reduce the totality of exercise to a minimum. Some I directed to change the qualities only, or the order, or the time. Some, however, I directed to change their whole form of exercise.

Galen classified exercises by speed and vigour and, in common with Celsus, highlighted the importance of integrating exercise with other hygienic components including massage, bathing, food, and rest. There was an interaction between movement and air with Celsus writing that 'it is better to walk in the open air than under cover; better under the shade of a wall or of trees than under a roof'.

Galen encouraged a consideration of 'opposites' to maintain the humoral balance suggesting that 'if the body has laboured too much on the previous day, do this by reducing the amount of exercises; if it has laboured too little, do this by increasing the amount of exercise'. Taking into account an individual's age mattered too, and for older people Galen recommended starting with a massage (with oils) followed by a gentle walk and some passive exercises.

Both Galen and Celsus expressed concerns about people adopting the exercise regimes of elite athletes rather than integrating movement into their day-to-day activities, Celsus wrote, 'the example of athletes should not be followed, with their fixed rules and immoderate labour' and Galen added that 'better are rowing, digging, reaping, javelin throwing, running, leaping, horse-riding, hunting, fighting with heavy arms, chopping wood, lifting and ploughing, and all other things done naturally; these are better than exercising in a wrestling school.'

In his short book *De parvae pilae exercitio* (On Exercise With a Small Ball), Galen's rationale underlying his theory was that it was easy to do, could be undertaken individually or in company, presented the opportunity to exercise all or parts of the body, could be tailored to different ages and constitutions and, above all, it was safe.

Sleep

Ensuring sufficient sleep – neither too much nor too little – was a key element of a healthy lifestyle. It was recognised that there was a need to use the waking hours productively and to allow a period of calm in the transition between activity and sleep. The Romans knew that while it was natural to be awake during the day and asleep at night; pain, distress, psychological problems, symptoms of some physical ailments such as indigestion, or old age were common causes of insomnia.

To Galen, the more active the mind during the day, the better the chances of a good night's rest as the brain required sleep to recover. To help to get to sleep Galen recommended exercise, food and wine in addition to 'washing the head with copious hot baths'. Silence and fresh air were also invaluable aids to sleep as were occasional herbal treatments. There is evidence that lavender-filled pillows, chamomile drinks and lettuce were all used by the Romans to treat insomnia.

Oversleeping was also seen as 'against nature' and for those wishing to languish in bed the Emperor Marcus Aurelius wrote:

> At day's first light have in readiness, against disinclination to leave your bed, the thought that 'I am rising for the work of man'. Must I grumble at setting out to do what I was born for, and for the sake of which I have been brought into the world?... to carry out Nature's bidding?

Diet

In terms of diet, Celsus wrote that 'a surfeit is never of service, excessive abstinence is often unserviceable; if any intemperance is committed, it is safer in drinking than in eating. It is better to begin a meal with savouries, salads and such-like.' He also recognised that food and drink 'are of general assistance not only in diseases of all kinds but in preserving health as well'. To the Romans, adequate food and drink were vital to good health but the focus needed to be on those things that promoted health, strength, longevity and nourishment.

Celsus divided foods into three groups according to their overall characteristics. In the top class he placed bread, pulses, the meat from large game and large domesticated animals, large birds, 'sea monsters' (including whale), honey and cheese; in the middle category smaller game, birds, fish and pot herbs whose roots or bulbs were eaten; and, at the bottom, vegetables, fruit, olives, snails and shellfish.

Galen attributed certain imbalances of humours and qualities to consuming particular items. Foods and drinks producing excessive heat included onions, garlic, leeks and 'old or bitter wine'. The Hippocratic text *Regimen in Health*, the foundation for much of Galen's work on food and drink, advised people that, in winter (to balance the humours and qualities), they should eat as much as possible and drink as little as possible and that all meat eaten in winter must be roasted. As spring comes on, individuals could gradually drink more and move towards boiled meat rather than roasted, so that by the time of summer all meats are boiled.

But, in achieving balance, the seasons were not the only aspect that mattered. Regimens had to vary according to an individual's constitution, habits, and body type. Flabby individuals were advised to keep to 'dry' foods for most of the year to counteract the natural moistness of their qualities. In terms of habits, it was seen as dangerous to suggest a foodstuff, or a quantity of food, with which they were not familiar. Any diet also needed to take into account a person's age and, for infants, Galen wrote that 'mother's milk is very likely best', but that 'wine is most undesirable, so for old men it is most useful'. Achieving a balanced diet was a very complicated process!

Eating cooked food rather than raw food, and in particular bread and meat, was viewed as something that set the ancient Greeks and Romans apart from animals and other peoples. Further 'cooking' was considered to take place in the body using the person's innate heat. Food was thought to begin its transformation in the mouth before undergoing additional changes in the stomach and liver until it eventually became blood; a process termed concoction.

Towards the end of the first century, Plutarch, the philosopher and essayist, expressed concerns that Romans no longer suffered from the diseases of want and deprivation but were now beset with diseases of luxury. Seneca also wrote how he became:

> enthusiastic about keeping the appetites for food and drink firmly in their place... I came to give up oysters and mushrooms for the rest of my life (for they are not really food to us but titbits which induce people who have already had as much as they can take to go on eating – the object most desired by gluttons and others who stuff themselves with more than they can hold – being items which will come up again as easily as they go down).

Excretions

It was thought that the unusable residues of concocted food and drink (superfluities) produced in different parts of the body would lead to humoral imbalances. There were three points of excretion: the rectum for dry/solid superfluities, the urinary bladder for wet/liquid superfluities and the skin for wet and vaporous superfluities through sweat and imperceptible transpiration.

Dietary adjustments and exercises were often recommended to manage individuals with retained superfluities. Some people were also purged by, for example, phlebotomy, bathing (to encourage sweating), the use of laxatives or eliciting vomiting.

Affections of the soul

In the Roman world the distinction between physical and mental wellbeing was much more blurred than is the case today. Looking after the psyche – the soul – was viewed as integral to the care of the body and it was a key element of Galen's *Hygiene* alongside movement, pure air, sleep and diet.

Many Romans citizens – in addition to physicians such as Galen – were seeking after a philosophy of life. Their desire was to achieve tranquillity by addressing both the prevention and the treatment of a range of psychological disturbances. One approach popularised by Seneca, Epictetus and Marcus Aurelius and others that found favour in the early Roman Empire was Stoicism. The overriding aim was to replace negative emotions such as grief, anger and anxiety with positive emotions such as joy.

In the first of his six books on hygiene Galen wrote:

> Not a few men, however many years they were ill through the disposition of their souls, we have made healthy by correcting the disproportion of their emotions. No slight witness of the statement is also our ancestral god Aesculapius who ordered not

> a few to have odes written as well as to compose comical mimes and certain songs.

On the face of it, it might seem odd that such a rational individual as Galen was also interested in divine cures. But within the Roman world the focus was not simply about 'being cured' or 'surviving' but the broader concepts of 'healing' and 'growth'. These two sides of the therapeutic relationship might even be termed 'Hippocratic and Aesculapian'.

Pharmaceuticals

The major surviving sources of information on the pharmaceutical remedies being used during the first and second centuries are contained in the writings of Scribonius Largus (see Chapter 8), Dioscorides, Celsus, Pliny the Elder and Galen. Supplementary evidence is provided by inscriptions on the small stones used to emboss eye medications (collyrium stamps) in addition to occasional archaeological finds of actual drugs.

Dioscorides was a first century physician who served in the Roman army during the time of Nero. His military position and extensive travels provided opportunities for studying diseases in addition to collecting and identifying numerous pharmaceutical remedies. In his five books, which constituted *De materia medica,* he recorded many plants previously unknown to Greek and Roman physicians and tried to describe not only their qualities and remedial effects, but also something of their morphology, including roots, foliage and flowers. In all, he outlined 944 remedies of which 657 are plants or products derived from plants.

Pliny the Elder wrote about approximately 1,000 medicinal plants in his books *Naturalis historia* during the reigns of Vespasian and Titus. He was one of a group of writers who flourished in the early empire termed 'encyclopaedists'. Across several fields of human endeavour and achievement they took it upon themselves to collect, consolidate and comprehensively record all the available knowledge. Another first-century medical encyclopaedist, Celsus, was probably born about 25BC and lived under the reign of Tiberius. In his *De medicina,* he discussed around 250 medicinal plants in addition to a wide range of inorganic medications based on, for example, copper, aluminium, arsenic, zinc, calcium, lead, iron, antimony and sulphur. However, unlike Pliny, Celsus might have been a physician – he certainly demonstrated considerably greater technical understanding and a more critical approach to assessing information.

Galen wrote extensively about the use of drugs and his major pharmaceutical works were *The Properties of Simples, Antidotes* and two dealing with compound drugs. In all he lists around 440 different plants and 250 other substances used as remedies with, in many cases, a wealth of information on issues such as storage, use and application. The first medicines that had been developed by the ancients often consisted of a single ingredient, occasionally with an additive to counter any adverse effects such as a bitter taste or, perhaps, to improve appearance or preservation. But during the early Roman period – and especially by the time of Galen – the emphasis was much more on using compound medicines made up of more than one active ingredient.

The underlying humoral theory, applied by Galen to guide his pharmaceutical prescriptions, proposed that each substance being used for treatment had both basic and derivative qualities. The basic qualities were the same for anything: active qualities (hot and cold) or passive qualities (dry and moist). The derivative qualities concerned the observable effects of a substance (such as a medication) on the body: heating or cooling, drying or moisturising, but also actions such as mollifying, burning, purging, rotting or suppurating. In addition, it was necessary to consider the strength of the substance and whether it attracted a specific type of humour which it then expelled from the body (i.e. as in the case of purgatives or emetics). In applying this theoretical foundation to select an appropriate drug, the physician also had to ascertain the nature of a patient's imbalance and the intensity of any therapeutic intervention required.

Roman doctors were certainly more cautious in their use of medications than is the case today. Part of this reticence might have been around uncertainties about the precise nature of the ingredients that a physician was able to procure from a drug seller. In relation to opium, Scribonius Largus implored his readers to 'use that which comes from the pulp of the poppy flower, not from the leaves, which the pedlars of ointments make for a profit. The former is wrought with great labour in small quantities; the other is ground up without bother and found abundantly'.

Galen also went to extraordinary lengths to assure the quality of his ingredients including, for example, travelling to Lemnos to observe how the medicinal clays were collected, washed, separated, dried and formed into small, stamped seals.

Surgery

There are several stone-carved representations of surgical instrument collections on Roman funerary monuments and a wall painting from Pompeii of a wounded Aeneas clearly illustrates the removal of an arrowhead using forceps. Also, by the early years of the first century, an increasingly large number of distinctive, purpose-made, metal tools labelled as 'surgical' begin to appear in the archaeological record from military, civilian and religious sites. Their identification often rests on comparisons being made with descriptions contained in ancient medical texts.

However, although we might have a view about the role of a particular object in relation to modern surgical practice, whether it really served that purpose can sometimes be debatable. Today's doctors clearly perform a different spectrum of operations using some dissimilar surgical techniques than did their Roman predecessors. Moreover, the injuries sustained during battle in the ancient world would have been quite distinct from those encountered in modern warfare and obviously required different approaches. The absence of effective anaesthesia would have also been an important consideration for the Roman surgeon.

The repair of a simple flesh wound was probably the most performed surgical procedure in the ancient world. It would have been undertaken by doctors but also a range of other individuals, such as a family member or, in the case of the army, a fellow soldier. Basic surgical kits consisting of probes, hooks, forceps, needles, cautery tools and scalpels were certainly readily available. Such instruments have been found scattered widely across Pompeii indicating that, perhaps, minor surgical procedures could have been performed in variety of locations including homes and bathhouses. In more severe injuries, loss of blood was a particular concern and detailed accounts of methods to staunch haemorrhaging were provided by several Roman medical authors including Galen and Celsus. Sometimes blood vessels had to be clipped and tied off if the bleeding did not respond to elevation, local pressure or cautery.

As ancient medicine was built on different theories and ideas than is modern medical practice, some of the surgical procedures described by Roman authors would, perhaps, be labelled inappropriate or cosmetic today. Excision of the uvula was often undertaken by Roman surgeons but in the UK it is now rare; only occasionally being used as a component of an overall surgical approach to ameliorate snoring. The Romans viewed hair removal as an important approach to treating several diseases too and shaving knives could thus be considered potential surgical tools as well as razors. There is also evidence of treatment variations across the Roman Empire and Celsus stated that 'methods of practice differ according to the nature of localities, and that one method is required in Rome, another in Egypt, another in Gaul'.

Bathing and hydrotherapy

To the Romans, bath-houses were about improving general health and wellbeing in addition to specific healing. Ancient authors frequently recommended taking or avoiding baths, either hot or cold, not only as remedies for all sorts of ailments, but also for the preservation of health. Galen's writings are peppered with references to bathing for medical purposes and Celsus referred to baths fifty-six times in a remedial connection and eleven times in a preventive one.

In accordance with humoral theory, bathing was viewed as a way of regulating the balance to 'draw out corrupt humour and change the bodily habit', by means of heating, cooling, moistening or drying. In addition, Celsus emphasised the importance of sweating in addressing humoral excesses: 'sweating also is elicited in two ways, either by dry heat, or by the bath'. He also went on to discuss the appropriate and careful use of baths for patients with fevers in addition to a variety of more specific problems such as headaches, worm infestations, boils and liver abscesses. For fevers he viewed bathing as having two purposes: 'after fevers have been dissipated, it forms for a convalescent the preliminary to a fuller diet and stronger wine; at another time it actually takes off the fever'.

Pliny the Elder devoted Book 31 of his *Naturalis historia* to water and wrote about natural springs:

> Nowhere do they abound in greater number, nor offer a greater variety of medicinal properties than in the Gulf of Baiae; some being impregnated with sulphur, some with alum, some with salt, some with nitre, and some with bitumen, while others are of a mixed quality, partly acid and partly salt. In other cases, again, it is by their vapours that waters are so beneficial to man.

He then proceeded to discuss the use of specific waters – drunk, bathed in, or applied hot or cold – as remedies for infertility, urinary stones, wound healing, memory problems and male insanity. In terms of mechanisms of action, Vitruvius commented:

> Sulphur springs refresh muscular weakness by heating and burning poisonous humours from the body. Alum springs affect

> parts of the body which are dissolved by paralysis or some stroke of disease; they warm through the open pores and overcome the cold by the opposing power of the heat, and thus forthwith the diseased parts are restored to their ancient health.

Warm water bathing – heated naturally or artificially – was more generally recommended for a variety of conditions including joint and ligament problems, back pain, gout and digestive disorders. It was also suggested that warm baths helped to allow nutritious food to be assimilated.

Massage and rocking

In an extensive discussion of massage in his second book on hygiene, Galen considered it both a specific therapy as well as an adjunct to exercise. He provided a detailed account of massage categorising it by quality (i.e., hard/firm, soft/gentle, moderate) and quantity (i.e., little, much, moderate). More specifically he wrote:

> In the preparatory massage before exercises, which has the objective of softening the bodies, it is necessary for a quality midway between hard and soft to prevail, and to model everything in relation to that. The rubbings should be of various kinds with laying on and moving around of the hands, not only moving them from above downward and from below upward, but also sideways, crosswise, obliquely and circularly.

Celsus echoed Hippocrates and Asclepiades in recommending massaging for a wide variety of conditions stating that 'rubbing, if strenuous, hardens the body, if gentle, relaxes; if much, it diminishes, if moderate, fills out'. For example, 'prolonged headaches are relieved by rubbing of the head, although not at the height of the pain'.

Rocking, another recommendation of Asclepiades, was seen as: 'very suitable for chronic maladies which are already abating; it is also of service both for those who are now entirely free of fever, but cannot as yet themselves take exercise'. Celsus explained:

> The gentlest rocking is that on board ship either in harbour or in a river, more severe is that aboard ship on the high seas, or in a litter or even severer in a carriage: but each of these can be intensified or mitigated. Failing any of the above, the bed should be so slung as to be swayed.

Cupping and phlebotomy

Cupping was performed by applying cups to selected skin points and creating a sub-atmospheric pressure. In simple dry cupping, suction was used to draw the skin inside the vessel without any additions. Wet cupping was the application of a suction vessel after the skin had been cut in order to draw out blood as a means of balancing the humours in individuals with 'plethora'. Celsus wrote:

> There are two kinds of cups, one made of bronze, the other of horn. The bronze cup is open at one end, closed at the other; the horn one, likewise at one end open, has at the other a small hole. Into the bronze cup is put burning lint, and in this state its mouth is applied and pressed to the body until it adheres. The horn cup is applied as it is to the body, and when the air is withdrawn by the mouth through the small hole at the end, and after the hole has been closed by applying wax over it, the horn cup likewise adheres.

CHAPTER 4

Augustus: Health Profile

(63BC–AD14; Emperor from 27BC)

The Emperor Augustus was an important individual in the history of the Western World, transforming a somewhat chaotic Roman Republic into an orderly imperial autocracy.

Augustus' mother Atia was Julius Caesar's niece and, following the death of his father when he was aged 4, she re-married. For the next eight years Augustus was largely brought up by his maternal grandmother, Julia Minor, subsequently being adopted by Julius Caesar. Augustus himself married three times; firstly, to Claudia, then Scribonia and, finally, in 38BC, to Livia. He fathered one daughter, Julia the Elder, by Scribonia and Livia already had two sons from a previous marriage (Tiberius and Drusus the Elder).

An intense rivalry between Augustus and Mark Antony commenced following the assassination of Julius Caesar in 44BC. Eventually, together with Lepidus, they formed the second triumvirate, campaigning together at Philippi (42BC) in addition to liquidating their political opponents (the 'proscriptions'). Following the Battle of Actium in 31BC, Augustus eventually achieved supreme authority over the Empire but during his time as Emperor he had to face numerous challenges as detailed by Pliny:

> The many plots against his life; the deaths of his own [grand] children, of which he was accused, and his heavy sorrows, caused not merely by their loss; the adultery of his daughter, and the discovery of her parricidal designs; the insulting retreat of … Tiberius; … the want of money to pay his soldiers; the revolt of Illyria; … the pestilence that raged in the City; the famine in Italy … the slaughter of Varus.

The surviving ancient sources also paint a picture of a person troubled by fragile health with periods of significant illness. Perhaps linked to this, the Imperial succession was something that particularly concerned Augustus. Ironically, he outlived all his favoured candidates: Marcellus (nephew, died 23BC); Gaius Caesar (grandson, died AD4); and Lucius Caesar (grandson, died AD2).

Nowadays Augustus is viewed as an enigmatic figure and, according to Levick, 'remains one of the most impenetrable personalities of the ancient world'. As an adult, he metamorphosed from a bad-tempered and bloodthirsty adventurer into a respected statesman. In addition, he was content to delegate significant authority and responsibility to two men – Marcus Agrippa and Gaius Maecenas – for military, architectural, administrative and diplomatic issues.

For clarity, the name Augustus is used throughout this chapter (including within quotes from ancient sources), but it is important to appreciate that, prior to 27BC, he was also known as Octavius.

Healers and Healthcare

Antonius Musa, Augustus' personal physician is well-known from the historical record linked to his successful treatment of the seriously ill emperor in 23BC. He was handsomely rewarded for his efforts, with his statute being erected adjacent to that of the healing god Aesculapius. Pliny contrasts his success in treating Augustus against the failure of the imperial physician C. Aemilius, underlining the intense rivalry between doctors and medical sects at the time. Interestingly, Musa's brother Euphorbus was employed as a doctor for the king of Mauretania.

Suetonius mentioned a rather less reputable Augustan physician Glyco 'who was imprisoned on the charge of having applied poison to [Consul Pansa's] wound' following the Battle of Mutina in 43BC. The loss of both consuls in this engagement was politically and personally highly convenient for the young Augustus.

Livia, Augustus' third wife, had a particular interest in medicine and keeping healthy. Pliny commented that she 'lived to her eighty-second year, attributing her longevity to the wine of Pucinium, as she never drank any other'. The fourth-century medical author Marcellus Empiricus also detailed two recipes she had developed to treat throat inflammation and cold limbs. Some epitaphs discovered with a columbarium on the Via Appia in 1726 provide a rich source of information on the Augustan imperial household, including the large medical contingent overseen by Livia. There is evidence for fifteen individuals who were involved in some aspects of personal health care including doctors, midwives, nurses and pharmacists. Three of the physicians were probably generalists and slaves of Livia (Eros, Hyginus and Tyrannus) working alongside a chief physician (*supra medicos*) and those with more specialist roles in surgery (*medicus chirurgus*) or eye care (*medicus ocularius*).

As an aedile in Rome, Augustus' right-hand man Marcus Agrippa made significant improvements to the city's infrastructure that might have had some impacts on the public health throughout the Julio-Claudian period. These included renovating and reconstructing much of the Cloaca Maxima, overseeing the building of the Aqua Julia and the Aqua Virgo in addition to repairing other aqueducts and erecting baths (e.g. the Baths of Agrippa). In relation to individual wellbeing, the Porticos of Agrippa, Vipsania and Livia offered opportunities to exercise, to gaze on works of art (art therapy) and to read Greek and Latin literature in their associated libraries (bibliotherapy). The Gardens of Agrippa – left to the citizens of Rome together with his baths in Agrippa's will – enabled individuals to get in touch with nature and to experience pure air.

Health Record

General health

There is significant literary evidence that throughout his adult life Augustus suffered from health problems. For example, in the context of a speech delivered prior to the Battle of Actium, Mark Antony was reported by Cassius Dio as stating: 'about his deficiencies in general I do not need to speak precisely of in detail, but I will sum up the whole matter and say, what you also know, that he is a veritable weakling in body'.

In *The Life of Augustus*, Nicolaus of Damascus highlighted some concerns about the teenage Augustus' wellbeing:

> Although he had been legally enrolled in the list of adults, his mother prevented him from going outside of the house except to go where he used to go previously as a boy, and she compelled him to conduct his life as he had before (δίαιτάν) and to sleep in the same room where he had previously slept. Only by law was he an adult; in all other respects he was treated as a boy.

> Young Augustus desired to join him [Julius Caesar] on the campaign to become experienced in matters of war, but when he perceived that his mother was opposed, he yielded without objection. Caesar, out of goodwill for the boy, also made it clear that he was not inclined to have him join the campaign so that he would not harm his health by changing the daily routine of his weak constitution (ἐν ἀσθενεῖ σώματι μεταβαλὼν καὶ τὴν ὅλην ἕξιν φαύλως διατεθείη).

According to Wardle,[9] ἐν ἀσθενεῖ σώματι can also be translated 'in his weak body' and καὶ τὴν ὅλην ἕξιν φαύλως διατεθείη as to 'be poorly disposed in respect of his whole system/constitution'. Bellemore (1984) reads this final section as 'in case he put a strain upon his constitution by changing the daily routine of his understrength body' and Hall (1923) suggests 'lest he might bring illness to a weak body through changing his mode of life and thus permanently injure his health'. From these passages it seems clear that the young Augustus was viewed as being in delicate health (ἕξιν). Moreover, the noun 'δίαιτα' – which Toher (2016) and Bellemore (1984) term 'daily routine' and Hall (1923) translates as 'mode of life' – can also be taken to mean a 'prescribed manner of life' or a 'heath regimen'.

It is highly likely that the teenage Augustus was already following a specific health programme (probably including a set diet, tailored exercise plan and prescribed rest periods) and there were concerns that any alterations to this regimen might have adverse effects on his overall wellbeing. In humoral terms Augustus' lifestyle was being very carefully regulated from an early age to maintain his health in a state of *eukrasia*.

The official document – *Res Gestae Divi Augusti* ('the achievements of the deified Augustus') – that was drafted by Augustus shortly prior to 2BC, also made specific reference to his general health:

> The senate decreed that vows for my good health be performed by consuls and priests every four years. In accordance with these vows games have often been celebrated in my lifetime, sometimes by the four most eminent colleges of priests and sometimes by the consuls. Moreover all citizens in private and as a municipality have, with one accord, repeatedly offered prayers for my good health at all public feasts.

Two coinage issues also alluded to the health of Augustus:

Augustus' health and his coinage

Date of issue	**Reverse legend**	**Coin type & reference**
16BC	**PRO VALETVDINE CAESARIS SPQR** ('for the health of Caesar')	Aureus RIC1 Augustus 369
19-15BC	**IOVI VOT SVSC PRO SAL CAES AUG** ('prayers to Jupiter were undertaken for the health of Caesar Augustus')	Denarius RIC1 Augustus 57

It was traditional for vows to be made by the consuls each year for the welfare of the state, but the sheer number of prayers and vows that seem to have been offered on behalf of the adult Augustus as a single individual was unprecedented.

In terms of Augustus' health regimen, Suetonius furnished us with information on three elements:

> **Diet:** As for food he ate very little and for the most part was ordinary. He was very keen on second-class bread [*secundarium panem*], small fishes, hand-pressed cheeses made from cow's milk and green figs. He was also very sparing by nature as far as wine was concerned.
>
> **Exercise:** Immediately after the civil wars he gave up exercising with horses and weapons on the Campus Martius; at first he turned to pass-ball and bladder-ball, but soon did nothing more than ride and take walks; at the end of his turn he would run with frequent jumps in the air, while wrapped in a cloak or short blanket.
>
> **Rest:** After his midday meal he used to have a short rest…after dinner he used to retire to a small couch…then he would go to bed and sleep no more than seven hours at most, and not even that was uninterrupted as he would wake up three or four times during that stretch…he was often short of sleep and would doze off as he was being carried through the streets.

In general terms, Suetonius also reported:

> In the winter he used to protect himself with four tunics and a thick toga, an under-tunic, a woollen chest-protector, and wraps for his thighs and shins… He could not put up even with the winter sun and at home did not walk in the open air without

wearing a broad-brimmed hat. He protected his very fragile health with great care, above all by bathing rarely. For he would be rubbed with oil very frequently or would sweat next to a fire and then he would have water poured over him that was either lukewarm or tepid.

Illnesses

In his biography of Augustus, Suetonius wrote 'throughout his whole life he suffered several severe and dangerous illnesses'.

Reviewing all the available literary evidence it seems likely that Augustus experienced recurrent bouts of illness throughout adulthood, with four particularly significant episodes (termed **EP1**, **EP2**, **EP3** and **EP4**).

Augustus' health record

Dates	**Illnesses**
46-45BC	**EP1**: Initial illness
42-41BC	**EP2**: Sickness before, during and after the battles at Philippi
40BC	Lay sick for several days at Canusium
36BC	Prior to the Battle of Naulochus was suddenly overcome by a very deep sleep
33BC	Sickness curtailing the Dalmatian campaign
29BC	Persistent throat problems
29BC	Sickness during ceremony dedicating shrine to Julius Caesar
28BC	Taken ill at circus games and headed the procession of carts lying in a litter
25-23BC	**EP3**: Progression to a severe illness
13BC	Hoarseness
6BC	Developed sickness following the departure of Tiberius for Capri in self-imposed exile

Dates	Illnesses
AD8	Extreme fatigue related to age and physical weakness
AD2	Weak voice
AD13	Persistent weakness
AD14	**EP4**: Fatal illness and death

Suetonius also listed several other problems but attached no specific dates:

> His body is recorded as being covered with spots…and also certain calluses in many places, hardened like scaly patches, caused by the itching of his body… He was not as strong in his left hip, thigh and leg, with the result that he would often limp, but he was strengthened by a treatment of thongs and canes. Sometimes he felt that the index finger of his right hand was so weak that, when it was numb and contracted with cold, he could barely move it to write, even with the support of a horn fingerstall. He also complained about his bladder and its pain was only relieved when he had passed stones in his urine.

EP1: Initial Illness (46-45BC)

Both Velleius Paterculus and Suetonius reported that the teenage Augustus travelled to Spain to join Julius Caesar on campaign. But Suetonius also commented that he undertook the journey 'even though he was scarcely recovered from a major illness…following…over roads beset by enemy, with very few companions and even suffering a shipwreck'.

Greater detail on this initial illness episode is provided by Nicolaus of Damascus:

> Caesar wished the boy to become experienced in such liturgic offices as presiding over games. There were two theatres, the

> Roman one, in which Caesar presided, and the other a Greek theatre, where he entrusted the presentation of the games to him. Because the boy was eager to demonstrate his diligence and benevolence during the long, hot days and never departed until he concluded the spectacle, he fell ill, since he was young and inexperienced in such exertions. When he became seriously ill, everyone, and most of all Caesar, was fearful and anxious that his constitution (φύσις), might succumb. Every day either Caesar himself was there to encourage and cheer him or he sent his friends, and he did not allow the doctors to leave his side. Once, while Caesar was dining, a message arrived that Augustus had collapsed (ἔκλυτος) and was in a difficult way. Caesar leapt up and, without putting on his shoes, arrived where he was being treated. Full of anxiety, he was frantically questioning the doctors and sat with the boy himself, and when he revived Caesar was elated.

Subsequently, Nicolaus went on to report:

> When the boy had recovered from his illness and was out of danger but still weak physically, Caesar had to depart for the campaign on which he had previously intended to bring the boy but now did not, because of the illness that had befallen him. Therefore, after leaving many caretakers with him so that he would be supervised in a strict regimen (ἀκριβοῦς διαίτης φυλάττοιτο), and having given orders that the boy was to follow him if he recovered his strength, Caesar went off to the war... Having been left behind in Rome, Augustus first took care of his body with great self-discipline and quickly regained his strength and then departed the city for the army…and with incredible speed he completed the long trip.

No other information is available to cast more light on the nature of Augustus' illness but, it was clearly of significance given the requirement for close medical supervision by doctors, the need for him to be 'watched and guarded' to ensure compliance (φυλάττοιτο) with a 'precise/exact regimen' (ἀκριβοῦς διαίτης), the progression with deterioration and collapse (ἔκλυτος) in addition to the extended time course. Augustus probably fell ill towards the end of July 46BC and, by November, he was still not fit enough to travel to Spain with Julius Caesar. He did not reach Caesar until after the Battle of Munda which was fought on 17 March 45BC.

EP2: Sickness before, during and after the battles at Philippi (42-41BC)

The two battles at Philippi were significant military encounters pitting the forces of Mark Antony and Augustus against the leaders of Julius Caesar's assassination, Brutus and Cassius. The first engagement took place around 3 October and the second about three weeks later. Several ancient writers reported that Augustus was very unwell before, during and after the conflict; for example, Suetonius wrote: 'Having entered into his agreement with Antony and Lepidus, he ended the Philippi War also with two battles, although he was weak and sick [*invalidus atque aeger*].'

The weakness and sickness that had preceded Augustus' arrival on the battlefield was described by the Greek historian Appian:

> They knew that Antony was approaching, after leaving Augustus behind ill at Epidamus…when everything they had thought of was complete, and Augustus had arrived (although he was not yet well enough for battle, and was carried in a litter up to the fighting units of the army), he and his allies immediately deployed their army for battle.

This Greek historian and philosopher Plutarch in his *Life of Brutus* also detailed the health challenges faced by Augustus on his journey to Philippi:

> They almost captured his forces, too, since Augustus was delayed by sickness; and they would have done so had not Antony come to his aid with such astonishing swiftness that Brutus could not believe it. Augustus came, however, ten days later, and encamped over against Brutus, while Antony faced Cassius.

Cassius Dio provides an even more comprehensive description of the events:

> Augustus fell sick and was left behind at Dyrrachium, while Antony marched toward Philippi; and for a time he was a source of some strength to his soldiers, but after laying an ambush for some of the enemy when they were gathering grain and failing in his attempt, even he was no longer hopeful. Augustus heard of the situation and...therefore he made haste, though still sick.

Two contemporaries of Augustus – Valerius Maximus and Velleius Paterculus – paint a picture of the future Emperor's detailed involvement in the first Battle of Philippi, perhaps derived from Augustus' autobiography:

> His physician Artorius being asleep, the night before the day when the Romans fought against each other in the plains of Philippi, the appearance of Minerva told him to warn Augustus, then lying very ill, that notwithstanding his sickness he should not abstain from the battle. When Augustus heard this he caused himself to be carried in a litter into the field of battle, where, while he laboured above his strength for the victory, his camp was taken by Brutus.

> Then Augustus and Antony transported their armies to Macedonia, and met Brutus and Cassius in battle near the city of Philippi. The wing under the command of Brutus, after

> defeating the enemy, captured Augustus' camp; for Augustus was performing his duties as commander although he was in the poorest of health, and had been urged not to remain in camp by Artorius his physician, who had been frightened by a warning which had appeared to him in his sleep.

Moreover, even after the battles had been fought and Augustus was returning home (probably at the start of 41BC), he was, according to Appian, still extremely sick: 'As for Augustus his illness flared up again dangerously on his way back to Rome, at Brundisium, and a rumour circulated that he was actually dead.'

Greater clinical detail on Augustus' illness at Philippi was provided by Pliny the Elder: 'his illness at the Battle of Philippi; his flight, and his having to remain three days concealed in a marsh, though suffering from sickness, and, according to the account of Agrippa and Maecenas, labouring under a dropsy [*aqua subter cutem fusa turgidi*].' The information furnished by Agrippa and Maecenas – '*aqua subter cutem fusa turgidi*' – translated here as 'dropsy' – literally means 'water spread out under swollen skin'. It is a rare example of a physical sign linked to an illness affecting Augustus being described in the ancient sources.

Augustus' extreme anger and brutality following the victory at Philippi is worth noting too. Suetonius, despite his pro-Augustan stance, wrote:

> Nor did he show restraint in victory, but sent Brutus' head to Rome to be thrown at the foot of Caesar's statue and vented his rage against all the most distinguished prisoners with insulting language. For example, Augustus is said to have answered a man who begged him for a decent burial 'that will now be up to the birds'; and he ordered others, a father and son who were asking for their lives, to cast lots or play morra, so that one of them could get their wish, and he watched them both die, since the son

> committed suicide after his father had been killed because he had offered himself up. As a consequence, all…greeted Antony respectfully as Emperor, but reviled Augustus to his face with the foulest of insults.

Cassius Dio also outlined some of the general concerns of the Roman population following the battle:

> Augustus was so prostrated by his sickness on the journey and during the voyage as to cause even the people in Rome to look for his death. They did not believe, however, that he was lingering so much by reason of ill health as because he was devising some mischief, and consequently they expected to suffer every possible injury. … During this delay of Augustus' all sorts of stories were current and all sorts of feelings resulted from them. For example, some spread a report that he was dead and caused pleasure to many people; others said he was planning some evil and filled numerous persons with fear. Therefore some proceeded to hide their property and to protect themselves, and others considered in what way they might possibly make their escape. Others, and they were the majority, being unable even to devise a plan by reason of their excessive fear, prepared to meet a certain doom.

The Roman socio-cultural context is distinct from ours with different ideas about acceptable levels of anger and aggression. However, the concluding comment made by Suetonius detailing the actions of Augustus and Mark Antony suggests a very significant difference between their responses to opponents.

EP3: Progression to a severe illness (25-23BC)

A useful overview of Augustus' illnesses during this period was provided by Cassius Dio.

25BC (Spring)
Augustus opened hostilities against the Astures and the Cantabri simultaneously and led the campaign himself. However, these tribes would neither surrender…nor would they come to close quarters...Augustus fell ill from the fatigue and anxiety caused by these conditions and retired to Tarraco, where he remained in weak health.

25BC
When the marriage of his daughter Julia was taking place in Rome and Augustus was unable through illness to attend at that time, he deputed Agrippa to conduct the celebrations in his absence.

24BC
The news arrived that Augustus was approaching the city, his return having been delayed by his illness.

23BC
Augustus became consul for the eleventh time with Calpurnius Piso as his colleague, and was then taken ill, this time so seriously that there appeared to be no hope of recovery. At any rate, he arranged all his affairs as if he were at the point of death, and gathered around him the officers of state and the most prominent senators and knights…and handed his ring to Agrippa. He had become too weak to deal with even the most urgent matters, but a certain Antonius Musa restored him to health by means of cold baths and cold potions.

Suetonius also focused specifically on the events of 23BC:

> Throughout his whole life he suffered several severe and dangerous illnesses; in particular after the conquest of Cantabria

> he was reduced to despair because his liver was damaged by catarrhal discharges and was forced to undergo an unprecedented and dangerous method of treatment: because hot poultices had not worked, on the advice of Antonius Musa he was forced to take a cold cure.

It is also helpful to reproduce the complete Latin entry for this section as it will be examined in some detail within Chapter 5: '*Graves et periculosas valitudines per omnem vitam aliquot expertus est; praecipue Cantabria domita, cum etiam destillationibus iocinere vitiato ad desperationem redactus contrariam et ancipitem rationem medendi necessario subiit; quia calida fomenta non proderant, frigidis curari coactus auctore Antonio Musa*'.[10]

Based on these two sources it seems highly likely that the years 25-23BC were dominated by another serious period of illness affecting Augustus. During the earlier part of that decade there were also references to throat problems (29BC), sickness during the dedication of Julius Caesar's shrine (29BC) in addition to an episode of debilitating illness at the circus games (28BC).

It is also of interest that, according to Tacitus, Augustus' second wife Livia was probably travelling with him at this time: 'Princes not infrequently had to visit the remote parts of the empire. How often had the deified Augustus travelled to west and east with Livia for his companion.' As mentioned earlier, Livia had a particular interest in dietetics or regimen to preserve or to maintain health and was also keen on various herbal remedies.

Augustus was clearly significantly debilitated after the illness episode of 23BC. Suetonius commented, 'he twice thought about handing back the state: … the second time, exhausted by a long illness, he even summoned the magistrates and senate to his house and handed over an account of the state of the empire.'

EP4: Fatal illness and death (AD14)

The clinical events preceding Augustus' death on 19 August AD14 were described by Suetonius in the following extracts:

> So, as he was about to send Tiberius off to Illyricum and to accompany him as far as Beneventum, when litigants detained him in giving judgements, he cried out that he would stay in Rome no longer, even if everything sought to delay him. This saying was itself soon numbered among the omens. Once he had begun the journey he went as far as Astura and from there, contrary to his usual practice, took a ship at night, using the opportunity of a breeze; this was the cause of an illness that began with diarrhoea [*causam valitudinis contraxit ex profluvio alvi*].

> Soon he crossed over to Naples, although even then his bowels were weak with intermittent attacks [*etiam tum infirmis intestinis morbo variante*]. Nonetheless he watched the whole of the quinquennial gymnastic competition that had been instituted in his honour and set off with Tiberius as far as the destination that had been agreed upon. But, as he was returning, his condition worsened and he finally took to his bed in Nola; he called back Tiberius from his journey, kept him for a long time in private conversation, and thereafter paid no attention to any business of importance.

Augustus' final journey from Rome to Nola via Beneventum probably took around sixteen days with stops at Capri and Naples on route. Subsequently it is estimated that Augustus spent a week at Nola before dying on 19 August.

From the description provided by Suetonius, Augustus' first symptom was '*profluvio alvi*' (translated as 'diarrhoea') which commenced shortly after departing from Astura around 26 July. It seems likely that the problem did not settle as, by the time he crossed over to Naples (1–4 August), Suetonius wrote '*infirmis intestinis morbo variante*' (translated as 'his bowels were weak with intermittent attacks').

Suetonius' use of '*profluvio alvi*' is consistent with Celsus who, in *De Medicina*, adopted the words *profluvium* and *profusio* with *alvi* to mean diarrhoea. Langslow suggests a more literal translation of '*infirmis intestinis morbo variante*' – 'his bowels weak as the disease came and went'.[11]

Associated with the bowel problems, Suetonius highlighted a possible episode of delirium too – 'before he breathed his last, he gave only one sign of having lost his mind, in that he took sudden fright and complained that he was being snatched away by forty young men'.

The events leading to Augustus' death were also mentioned by Tacitus, Velleius Paterculus and Cassius Dio. Tacitus statement that 'the health of Augustus deteriorated', perhaps lends some support to Suetonius' account that the Princeps' demise was not a sudden event. Velleius Paterculus, Tacitus and Cassius Dio also concur with Suetonius in stating that Augustus died at Nola. Moreover, Velleius provided some additional details that, in broad terms, echoed Suetonius:

> We now come to the crisis which was awaited with the greatest foreboding. Augustus Caesar had dispatched his grandson Germanicus to Germany to put an end to such traces of the war as still remained, and was on the point of sending his son Tiberius to Illyricum to strengthen by peace the regions he had subjugated in war. With the double purpose of escorting him on his way, and of being present at an athletic contest which the Neapolitans had established in his honour, he set out for Campania. Although he had already experienced symptoms of growing weakness and of a change in his health for the worse, his strong will resisted infirmity and he accompanied his son. Parting from him at Beneventum he went to Nola. As his health grew daily worse, and he knew full well for whom he must send

> if he wished to leave everything secure behind him, he sent in haste for his son to return. Tiberius hurried back and reached the side of the father of his country before he was even expected. Then Augustus, asserting that his mind was now at ease, and, with the arms of his beloved Tiberius about him, commending to him the continuation of their joint work, expressed all his readiness to meet the end if the fates should call him.

Thus, Augustus gradually travelled to Nola, where he died, and some of the journey was completed by sea. A separate passage from Suetonius is also helpful in detailing the Emperor's unhurried travelling habits: 'He would travel in a litter, normally at night and in slow, easy stages, so that it took him two days to get to Praeneste or Tibur. If he could reach anywhere by sea, he would rather sail.'

Injuries

Aside from illnesses, Augustus sustained some combat injuries. For example, according to Suetonius, in 34BC and 35BC: 'In the Dalmatian War he was even wounded: in one battle he was struck on the right knee by a stone and in another he was wounded in the leg and both arms by the collapse of a bridge.'

Appian also mentioned the bridge episode, adding 'he had almost crossed…when the army in shame leapt up en masse. Overloaded, the bridge collapsed…Caesar was struck on the right leg and both arms, but nonetheless immediately climbed the tower with his insignia and showed that he was unharmed.'

CHAPTER 5

Augustus: Health Report

Modern historians and physicians have suggested a range of physical diagnoses to account for Augustus' health problems. For Albert Esser (1958) the broad category of 'circulatory problems' could be used to explain most of Augustus symptoms and signs. Others, such as Anthony Everitt (2006), have sought greater diagnostic precision – for example, assigning a major episode of illness as a teenager to a 'severe bout of sunstroke'.

During the third decade BC, Augustus was particularly unwell and, based on the words '*iocinere vitiato*' (translated as 'liver damage') used by Suetonius, it has been argued that he had chronic hepatitis. Typhoid has been suggested for this episode too in appreciation of the death of Augustus' nephew Marcellus around the same time. Moreover, the Imperial physician, Musa, used cold water therapies on Augustus that were in vogue for treating typhoid in the nineteenth century; something that has been cited as supporting evidence. Augustus' illnesses have also been labelled as stress-related or feigned. According to Werner Eck (2007), 'it would not be surprising if the demands on him were the cause of the serious illness he developed in the late spring of 23BC.'

Based on Augustus' health profile (see Chapter 4) this chapter will first seek to carefully analyse and evaluate the evidence assembled before generating any diagnostic conjectures. Particular attention will be given to the potential for magnification, minimisation, misclassification and distortion of the historical clinical data.

Analysis and evaluation

'Magnification' is about assessing if any of the health problems reported as affecting Augustus might have been fabricated or exaggerated.

For example, caution needs to be exercised in relation to some of the health-related comments of Nicolaus of Damascus. As a teenager, Augustus would have been particularly keen to emphasise his close relationship to his great uncle (and adoptive father) Julius Caesar. Nicolaus' use of minor details to enhance the significance of health events is particularly intriguing, such as Caesar running barefoot/shoeless to the sick bed of Augustus.

Crook wrote, 'Scepticism is common amongst historians about the illnesses that punctuated the first forty years…they were, it is supposed, psychological reactions to tense situations or even fraudulent and calculated.'[12] A specific suggestion has been made that Augustus' brief episode of sickness during 6BC was designed to dissuade Tiberius from retreating into self-imposed exile on Capri (see Chapter 6). Feigning is defined as the intentional production of false or grossly exaggerated physical or psychological symptoms, motivated by external incentives. Adopting a sick role is certainly a convenient way to avoid some prolonged social, religious or political obligations as in the case of the dedication ceremony (29BC) or the circus games (28BC). But, taking the health record as a whole, it seems unlikely that Augustus was constantly feigning or exaggerating illnesses. The lengths of incapacity, the lack of any obvious external benefit to being sick in most situations and Augustus' diligence in following recommended treatments suggest that the illnesses he was experiencing were genuine. There is also some consistency across the historical record in respect of the broad nature of Augustus' underlying illness. Also, physical signs – such as the oedema reported at Philippi – are very difficult to falsify and Pliny explicitly reports that this information was provided by Agrippa and Maecenas rather than simply being derived from Augustus. It is also difficult to feign battle injuries.

'Minimisation' is about assessing if any of the health problems reported as affecting Augustus might have been understated.

The official version of the battles at Philippi was recorded in *Res Gestae Divi Augusti*: 'Those who killed my father I drove into exile by way of the courts of law, exacting retribution for their crime and afterwards I defeated them twice in battle while they were making war upon the state.' This statement is intriguing as it ignores the role of Mark Antony, the names of Augustus' opponents as well as the illness and incapacity reported by several ancient authors.

Augustus wrote an autobiography – the *Commentarii de vita sua* – and, although little remains of this work, it is generally agreed that it would have been one of the sources consulted by many of the ancient authors. It has been suggested that the purpose of the *Commentarii* was to justify Augustus' actions to his contemporaries, while the *Res Gestae Divi Augusti* had a wider role in laying out his achievements for posterity. Some consider the *Res Gestae Divi Augusti* propaganda, with the section dealing with the events at Philippi being a good example of how Augustus might have been somewhat economical with the truth.

Valerius Maximus and Velleius Paterculus were, perhaps, echoing the words in Augustus' autobiography by choosing to frame his illness as an adversity that he had to overcome. The former wrote:

> His physician Artorius being asleep, the night before the day when the Romans fought against each other in the plains of Philippi, the appearance of Minerva told him to warn Augustus, then lying very ill, that notwithstanding his sickness he should not abstain from the battle [*moneret ne propter adversam valitudinem proximo proelio non interesset*]. When Caesar heard this he caused himself to be carried in a litter into the field of battle, where, while he laboured above his strength for the victory, his camp was taken by Brutus'.

The phrase '*moneret ne propter adversam valitudinem proximo proelio non interesset*' is important in the advice given to Augustus against non-participation in the battle despite his sickness. This is also mentioned by Velleius Paterculus:

> Then Caesar and Antonius transported their armies to Macedonia, and met Brutus and Cassius in battle near the city of Philippi. The wing under the command of Brutus, after defeating the enemy, captured Caesar's camp; for Caesar was performing his duties as commander although he was in the poorest of health, and had been urged not to remain in camp by Artorius his physician, who had been frightened by a warning which had appeared to him in his sleep.

Augustus himself was awarded a *clipeus aureus* (golden shield) by the Senate and the people of Rome in 27BC highlighting the qualities that he embodied: *virtus, clementia, iustitia, pietas* (translated as 'manliness', clemency, justice and piety). But to the Romans the term '*virtus*' meant more than simply military success and bravery in battle as had been the case for the Greeks. Perhaps a comment by Quintilian written around 95 serves to encapsulate something of the contemporary Roman thinking about '*virtus*', that included overcoming physical and psychological challenges:

> Who will teach courage, justice, loyalty, self-control, simplicity, and contempt of grief and pain better than men like Fabricius, Curius, Regulus, Decius, Mucius and countless others? For if the Greeks bear away the palm for moral precepts, Rome can produce more striking examples of moral performance, which is a far greater thing.

Although it is highly likely that Augustus was suffering from a genuine illness at Philippi, the problem was how to counter any negative views about his role in the battle as a result of his sickness. Perhaps overcoming health challenges was initially portrayed as a heroic virtue but as time passed and memories faded, its significance was downplayed. Ignoring both Mark Antony's role and the illness was certainly a convenient way to magnify Augustus' own importance in the conflict at Philippi.

Throughout history, some illnesses and symptoms have also acquired metaphorical meanings. In the ancient literature severe bowel symptoms, for example, were often used to characterise an unpleasant individual. Concerning the deteriorating health of Herod the Great in 4BC, Josephus wrote: 'Now Herod's distemper greatly increased on him after a severe manner, and this by God's judgement upon him for his sins...his entrails were ulcerated, and the chief violence of his pain lay on his colon.' Within Rome, according to Plutarch, Sulla's immorality, injustice and unfairness also had adverse consequences for his bowels: 'By this mode of life he aggravated a disease which was insignificant in its beginnings, and for a long time he knew not that his bowels were ulcerated. This disease corrupted his whole flesh.'

Thus, in relation to Suetonius' somewhat benign and modest description of Augustus' terminal bowel problems, it is important to entertain the possibility that the symptoms might have been downplayed. According to Nutton, 'a sudden massive evacuation leading to death is the sign of a bad monarch'[13] and Suetonius would have been keen to steer well clear of any such metaphors.

'Misclassification' is about assessing if any of the health problems reported as affecting Augustus might have been incorrectly categorised due to, for example, socio-cultural or medical differences between the ancient and modern worlds.

Concerning Augustus' illness during **EP3**, two brief extracts from Suetonius (see Chapter 4) – '*iocinere vitiato*' and '*cum etiam destillationibus*' – are worthy of detailed consideration alongside the contemporary illness suffered by Marcellus.

Iocinere vitiato

In relation to '*iocinere vitiato*' (translated as 'liver damage'), Badian wrote that it 'should not be dissociated from the attack he suffered in Spain in 25BC … the series most obviously suggests a chronic hepatitis, either picked up in Spain or (if we ascribe some of his earlier bouts of illness to it) perhaps going back even further.'[14]

Although it does not seem unreasonable to link together Cassius Dio's health-related comments from 25-23BC, Badian's suggestion of chronic hepatitis is much more tenuous. More specifically, there is no mention of any other liver-related symptoms by Suetonius, aside from stating that it was caused by *destillatio* (see below). Similarly, Cassius Dio only refers to fatigue and anxiety (ἔκ τε τοῦ καμάτου καὶ ἐκ τῶν φροντίδων), symptoms that do not indicate any specific organ being affected.

If there was liver dysfunction then reference might have been made to other symptoms and signs such as anorexia, nausea/vomiting, pain or jaundice in addition to changes in the colour of the urine/stool. For example, Celsus wrote:

> Disease of … the liver, is sometimes chronic, sometimes acute… There is severe pain in the right part under the praecordia, which spreads to the right side, to the clavicle and arm of that side; at times there is also pain in the right hand, there is hot shivering. In a grave case there is vomiting of bile; sometimes the patient is nearly choked by hiccough. Such are the signs when acute; but in a more chronic case, where there is suppuration within the liver, and the pain at times ceases, at times is intensified.

However, although greater detail might be expected in the medical writings of Celsus, it is important to appreciate that Suetonius and Cassius Dio were biographers and historians drawing on earlier written sources. Therefore, they could, perhaps, be forgiven for considering that the information they proffered was sufficient to emphasise the seriousness of Augustus' predicament. But, even if we accept the accuracy of Suetonius' words, they need to be considered in context. There is little doubt that the ancient and medieval worlds were much more 'hepatocentric' than is the case today with the liver being viewed as the repository of life. According to Galen, digested food was thought to be absorbed from the gut, taken up by the mesenteric veins and turned into blood within the liver for distribution around the body via the branches of the venae cavae. Moreover, he argued that the liver and its subsidiary organs worked together to produce and store three of the four humours of the body: blood (liver), yellow bile (gall bladder) and black bile (spleen).

It has been suggested that the ancient phrase 'hit in the liver' was equivalent to our modern 'strike at the heart'. Both are metaphors for attacking the most important part of an individual or an organisation. In the *Iliad*, liver injuries were viewed as universally fatal, for example: 'Eurypylus…hurled with his shining spear, and smote Apisaon…in the liver below the midriff' and Achilles 'smote [Tros] upon the liver with his sword'. The reference to the piercing of Jesus' side with a lance in John's Gospel and in later imagery (e.g. Caravaggio *The Incredulity of St Thomas*, 1601) also appears to be hepatocentric. It took until the seventeenth century before the true physiological function of the liver began to be appreciated based on the works of individuals such as William Harvey and Thomas Bartholin.

As a result of hepatocentricism it might be argued that, at the time of Augustus, an individual who was significantly ill with non-specific symptoms would probably be categorised with liver problems if there were no clear pointers to other conditions or organs. Even if there was pain in the right upper abdomen it could be argued that this would be much more likely to be ascribed to the liver than to, perhaps, the bowel, the heart, the kidneys, the chest or the endocrine glands. Galen himself demonstrates a fixation on the liver when he described his assessment of a feverish patient who was being treated by another physician:

> Just when I entered [the house] I encountered a person who carried from the bed chamber to the toilet a pan containing a thin bloody serum similar to the watery fluid of freshly slaughtered meat, which is a definite indication of a disease of the liver… When I noticed that a little cooking pot, standing on the window, contained a preparation of hyssop in water and honey, I came to the conclusion that this physician believed [his patient] suffered from pleurisy, because he had pain in the area of the false ribs as it sometimes occurs during inflammation of the liver. Because he had this and his respiration was fast and shallow and he felt irritated by brief coughing spells, [the physician] had prepared hyssop in water and honey.

Galen concluded that liver disease had been misdiagnosed as pleurisy whereas, to a modern physician, the symptoms are much more suggestive of a lung disorder. Also in relation to the 'thin bloody serum' was it expectorated bloody phlegm, a bloody/watery stool or from a medical phlebotomy?

As a result of this discussion, it is important to entertain the possibility that Suetonius' reference to '*iocinere vitiato*' might bear little or no relation to our modern understanding of liver damage.

Cum etiam destillationibus

According to Lewis and Short (2020), the noun, '*destillatio*', is translated as 'a dripping down or distilling.' From a medical perspective, it is often viewed as being synonymous with modern day catarrh, a benign condition.

However, Suetonius adopts the plural ablative form in suggesting that Augustus' liver had been specifically damaged *by means of* these catarrhal discharges. Moreover, a careful analysis of the medical writings of Celsus demonstrates his use of this noun in several circumstances (see Appendix 1). What is clear from these extracts is that the '*destillatio*' suffered by Augustus might have a totally different medical significance than is the case with the modern term catarrh. The various textual associations with, for example, *phthisis* and chronic/recurrent lung problems are particularly intriguing, as is the enhanced significance of the condition in thin or slender individuals.

In his writings, Pliny also used various forms of the noun *destillatio* and seems to echo Celsus in associating the condition with serious chest problems. For example, he recommended leek juice for the 'spitting of blood, moreover, for phthisis, and for chronic catarrhs [*sanguinem vero excreantibus et phthisicis et destillationibus longis*]' and 'cut leek for cough, catarrh of the chest, and affections of the lungs and of the trachea [*tussim et destillationes thoracis, pulmonis et arteriae vitia sanat*]'. He referred to 'catarrh of the chest' too – '*thoracis destillationibus*' – that was treated with raw egg yolk.

The philosopher Seneca also made an interesting analogy between the consequences of recurrent 'passions' and recurrent '*destillatio*' writing:

> Passions are objectionable impulses of the spirit, sudden and vehement; they have come so often, and so little attention has been paid to them, that they have caused a state of disease; just as a catarrh [*destillatio*] when there has been but a single attack and the catarrh has not yet become habitual, produces a cough, but causes phthisis when it has become regular and chronic.

Based on the Hippocratic writings, it was thought that '*destillatio*' could cause a displacement of corrosive humours forming a nodule – *phyma* – in the lung. Galen considered that such corrosion could then lead to coughing up of blood and/or lung tissue.

The illness of Marcellus

As a result of the successful treatment of Augustus, Antonius Musa achieved considerable prestige. Suetonius wrote: 'In honour of his doctor, Antonius Musa, through whose treatment he had recovered from a dangerous illness, they collected money and set up a statue near to that of Aesculapius'.

Cold water therapies immediately became very fashionable and even the poet Horace was obliged to follow the trend. But things did not go as smoothly as Musa would have liked, with the subsequent death of Marcellus. Cassius Dio wrote:

> Musa received a great deal of money from both Augustus and the senate, as well as the right to wear gold rings (for he was a freedman), and he was granted exemption from taxes, both for himself and for the members of his profession, not only those living at the time but also those of future generations. But it was fated that he who had taken to himself the functions of Fortune or Destiny should speedily be caught in her coils; for though Augustus had been saved in this manner, yet when Marcellus fell ill not long afterward and was treated in the same way by Musa, he died.

Marcellus' death has been put down to plague as suggested by Cassius Dio (although foul play by Livia was suspected in some people's minds):

> Livia, now, was accused of having caused the death of Marcellus, because he had been preferred before her sons; but the justice of this suspicion became a matter of controversy by reason of the character both of that year and of the year following, which proved so unhealthful that great numbers perished during them.

Plagues were not uncommon in Rome at this time, and this has conveniently been used to associate the illnesses of Augustus and Marcellus in 23BC. The two events were clearly linked together by Cassius Dio and the modern historian Anthony Everitt (2006) takes a similar view.

However, it is important to appreciate that the illnesses of the two individuals were separated by between three and six months. Augustus fell ill in the early summer (certainly before 1 July when he was well enough to resign as consul) whereas Marcellus became sick in the autumn, probably dying towards the end of the year. Although nothing survives detailing Marcellus' symptoms, there is little doubt that he had a number of enemies (aside from Livia as suggested earlier by Cassius Dio). The behaviour of Augustus in relation to Marcellus during 23BC was somewhat intriguing too. On his perceived deathbed, he passed the state papers to his colleague Piso and his ring to Marcus Agrippa. There was nothing for Marcellus. Also, the absence of any testimony from Marcellus at the subsequent trial of Marcus Primus – which could have proved tricky for the Emperor – was somewhat fortunate for Augustus!

The death of Marcellus remains mysterious, but I would suggest that whatever took him away – foul play or plague – was quite distinct from the illness that had affected Augustus earlier that same year.

'Distortion' is about assessing if any of the health problems reported as affecting Augustus might have been deliberately misreported or misrepresented by the ancient authors for, perhaps, political, socio-cultural or religious reasons.

The physical condition of an emperor was important as it could impact on their political or military ability to act. But illnesses could also showcase the emperor's responses to personal suffering and how the wrath or the favour of the gods was manifest. In relation to his illness at Philippi it has already been suggested that Augustus might have sought to reframe his response as a virtue. However, it also presented an opportunity to associate himself with the goddess Minerva in the context of a dream, as described by Cassius Dio:

> The physician who attended Caesar dreamed that Minerva commanded him to lead his patient, though still in poor health, from his tent and place him in the line of battle – the very means

> by which he was actually saved. For whereas in most cases safety is the lot of such as remain in the camp and within its ramparts, while it is dangerous to go into the midst of weapons and battles, this was reversed in the case of Caesar, since it was very manifestly the result of his leaving the intrenchments and mingling with the combatants that he survived, although by reason of his sickness he found it difficult to stand even without his arms.

For Suetonius, Augustus was an exemplar of the ideal emperor and, consequently, it seems likely that his account of the events leading up to his death would have been influenced by this perspective. Wardle argues that 'every detail contributes to a picture of the paradeigmatic death of the good emperor'[15] and that Augustus 'dies the perfect, controlled death that was the ideal of the Roman elite: the biographer is diligent both in what he excludes and in the details his account presents, to give the first princeps the perfect send-off'.[16]

Moreover, some elements of Suetonius' account might be interpreted as part of Augustus' spiritual journey to deification:

> When he was concluding the census on the Campus Martius in the presence of a large number of people, an eagle flew around him rather frequently and crossing over to a nearby temple sat above the first letter of the name Agrippa... Around the same time the first letter of his name was melted from the inscription on his statue by a lightning strike. The interpretation of this was that he would live for only a hundred days thereafter, the number which the letter C indicated, and that he would be numbered among the gods because 'aesar' [that is, the remaining part of the name Caesar] meant 'god' in Etruscan.

In the context of the journey from Capri to Naples Suetonius also reported: 'As he was sailing past the bay of Puteoli it chanced that passengers and crew of a ship from Alexandria which had only just put in, dressed in white, wearing garlands and offering incense, heaped upon him omens of good fortune and the highest praises.' It has been suggested that the whole of Augustus' voyage along the coast of Campania – including the stops at Capri and Naples – was imbued with religious and political symbolism. The episode in the bay of Puteoli shows Augustus receiving divine honours and, at Naples, he attended a festival that had been established in his honour.

Even the episode of possible delirium, when Augustus thought he was being taken away by a group of men, was transformed into a virtue by Suetonius. He suggested that it furnished the dying Augustus with an ability to prophesy: 'That too was more a piece of foresight than the diminution of his mind, as that was the very number of praetorian soldiers who carried his body in public.'

Intriguingly both Tacitus and Cassius Dio also reported on another journey undertaken by Augustus – shortly prior to death – to the island of Planasia (now Pianosa) between Italy and Corsica. This trip was not mentioned by either Suetonius or Velleius and the stated purpose was to visit his estranged grandson, Agrippa Postumus:

> The health of Augustus deteriorated. Some suspected his wife of foul play. For rumour had it that a few months earlier, with the knowledge of his immediate circle but accompanied only by Paullus Fabius Maximus, he had gone to Planasia to visit Agrippa Postumus; and that there had been a tearful display of affection on both sides that the young man seemed very likely to be received back into the home by his grandfather.

> So Augustus fell sick and died. Some suspicion attached itself to Livia concerning the cause of his death, because he had secretly sailed over to the island of Planasia to visit Agrippa Postumus, and it appeared that he was about to become completely reconciled with him. Livia was afraid, some people allege, that Augustus might bring him back to make him emperor, and so

> smeared with poison some figs which were still ripening on trees from which Augustus was in the habit of picking the fruit with his own hands. She then ate those which had not been smeared and offered the poisoned fruit to him. At any rate, he fell sick from this or from some other cause.

There has been considerable speculation about the veracity of Augustus' journey to visit Agrippa Postumus as well as Livia's role in the emperor's death. Following a detailed and careful analysis Charlesworth considered it very unlikely that 'the voyage to Planasia – at least fifty miles from the nearest port – took place in the last four months of Augustus' life'[17].

There is little doubt that immediately following Augustus' death considerable political manoeuvring took place with both supporters and enemies of Livia and Tiberius putting forward different versions of events. Such information would have become available to Tacitus and Cassius Dio with the latter concluding 'this, at any rate, is the account by most writers, including the most trustworthy ones'. Also, according to Charlesworth, 'the smearing of figs upon the tree has an air rather of Alice in Wonderland…and why trouble to poison Augustus at all when her son's succession was certain?'

Diagnostic Conjectures

Chronic Lung Disorder

Based on the careful analysis of two extracts from Suetonius: '*cum etiam destillationibus*' and '*iocinere vitiato*', my hypothesis is that Augustus was suffering from a lung disorder in 23BC (perhaps giving him symptoms in the right lower chest/upper abdomen that could have suggested liver problems to an ancient physician). The translation of '*redactus contrariam et ancipitem rationem medendi necessario subiit*' indicates that Augustus was forced to 'undergo an unprecedented and dangerous method of treatment' that, according to Cassius Dio, involved 'ψυχρολουσίαις καὶ ψυχροποσίαις', literally translated as 'a bathing in cold water and a drinking of cold water'.

Additional understanding of Augustus' condition might be derived from the words '*contrariam et ancipitem rationem medendi*' by considering how the Hippocratic theory of humours and qualities impacted on the medical treatments being selected for Augustus by his physicians. In his commentary on Hippocrates, Galen wrote:

> Diseases differ from each other with respect to hot and cold, wet and dry, and the treatment is to chill what is hot, and dry out what is wet; and similarly to heat what is cold and make wet what is dry. Furthermore, he proposes that, of the natures pertaining to men before these diseases arise, some natures are hot, and some are cold, some wet and some dry, and he supposes time and place to differ from each other in the same way.

Moreover the Hippocratic 'theory of opposites' could be applied in seeking to rectify matters. For example, if a patient was 'cold' with an excess of the humour 'phlegm', then the recommended treatments (i.e. foods, exercises, bathing, medicines or physical therapies) would be specifically selected to 'warm' them or apply heat to their affected parts. A Hippocratic-schooled physician might also believe that some of the excess phlegm had separated from the humoral mixture and was now moving around the body affecting organs such as, for example, the liver. In such circumstances and in the words of Celsus 'all cold things must be especially avoided; for nothing is more harmful to the liver'.

However, at the time of Augustus an alternative 'atomic' medical theory was becoming more acceptable within Rome based on the teachings of Asclepiades of Bithynia. It is even possible that Augustus' wife Livia was interested in such an approach and Pliny specifically commented that Augustus' physician at this time – Antonius Musa – had been a pupil of Asclepiades. According to Asclepiades, within healthy individuals, fragile corpuscles travelled through undefined channels (pores) distributed throughout the body. Diseases occurred when this process was disrupted by, perhaps, constriction or relaxation of the pores. Pliny explained:

> The ancient system of medicine remained unshaken … until, one Asclepiades, a professor of rhetoric … suddenly abandoned rhetoric for medicine. A man who neither had practised it nor knew anything of remedies that call for sharp eyes and personal experience … reducing the whole of medicine to the discovery of causes, made it a matter of guesswork. He recognised especially five principles of general application: fasting from food, in other cases abstinence from wine, massage, walking, and the various kinds of carriage-rides … he would prescribe cold water; and, to win for himself the surname of cold-water giver.

Scarborough states that 'to Asclepiades, the whole concept of the humours was irrelevant in medicine, and drugs remained their own substance in all pharmaceutical therapy'.[18] Pliny detailed how applying Asclepiades' theory could, perhaps, reverse the approach to treatment by overturning the humoral/quality-based theory of opposites: 'Antonius Musa…with the support of the late Emperor Augustus, whose life in a dangerous illness had been saved by reversing the treatment'.

Pliny also furnished us with two specific examples:

> Musa we have mentioned as the saviour of the life of the late Emperor Augustus…first adopted the plan of bracing the body by copious douches of cold water after the bath. Before this the custom was to bathe in hot water only, as we find that it is also in Homer.

> Indeed [lettuces] have a cooling quality, and consequently are acceptable in summer. They relieve the stomach of distaste for

> food and promote appetite. At all events it is stated that the late lamented Augustus in an illness, thanks to the sagacity of his doctor, Musa, was cured by lettuce, which had been refused him by the excessive scruples of his previous doctor, Gaius Aemilius.

I would argue that Suetonius is alluding to this underlying theoretical dilemma in his use of the words '*redactus contrariam*' (received the opposite) followed by '*ancipitem rationem medendi*' (a remedy of uncertain rationale). Importantly, in attempting to identify Augustus' underlying illness, this difference of opinion is consistent with the Emperor suffering from a cold dyskrasia, most probably with an excess of phlegm suggesting a lung-related disorder.

In addition to this specific episode in 23BC, there are possible lung-related events reported in Augustus' health record. In 29BC, according to Suetonius' *De Poetis*, he suffered with a prolonged throat and voice problem, requiring a break in his journey for several days highlighting the significance of the episode: 'When Augustus was returning after his victory at Actium and lingered at Atella to treat his throat, Vergil read the *Georgics* to him for four days in succession, Maecenas taking his turn at the reading whenever the poet was interrupted by the failure of his voice.' In 13BC Cassius Dio reported, 'After this he summoned the senate. Because he was suffering from hoarseness he did not address them himself, but handed his text to the quaestor to read'. Throat problems and dysphonia were also noted in 12AD when Cassius Dio mentioned that Augustus wrote a letter but 'did not read it out himself, since he could not now make himself heard'. And Suetonius commented that 'sometimes he spoke to people through a herald if his throat was weak.'

Although most of the other illness episodes are described in very general terms, including non-specific symptoms such as fatigue and weakness, there is nothing in the assembled medical record inconsistent with a chronic lung problem having troubled him throughout his adult life.

Intriguingly, in his book, *De antidotis*, Galen refers to a remedy developed by the Greek physician and pharmacologist Damocrates (first century AD):

> Another very good [treatment] for those who suffer from phthisis. And for those spitting blood, and for those who are imperceptibly feverish, and those who have a weak chest … They say that Augustus himself used it with pleasure and became healthy in a short time, as he was experiencing distress in his ribs and chest.

Pliny also commented on the curative value of bitter vetch for Augustus, which was used for a variety of lung problems:

> Bitter vetch [*ervi*] also is not difficult to cultivate. This needs weeding more than the vetch; and it too has medicinal properties, indeed the fact that his late Majesty Augustus was cured by it stands on record in his own letters'.

Although Pliny does not specifically mention its use for cough this was certainly the case in cattle according to Columella as it can 'dispel the most inveterate cough. The same effect is produced by bitter-vetch without its husk pounded up with an equal portion of toasted barley and poured down the throat in the manner of a drench'.

Within Galen's *De antidotis* remedies containing bitter vetch for catarrh, hoarseness and coughing blood were detailed and also linked to Antonius Musa.

In relation to phthisis, Celsus wrote: 'The malady usually arises in the head, thence it drips into the lung; there ulceration supervenes … pus is expectorated, sometimes blood-stained … recourse should be had to moderate exercise, walking in particular, and also to gentle rubbing. The bath is unsuitable.' This statement is important, particularly with reference to the comment about bathing, as Suetonius remarked that Augustus bathed rarely but would 'be rubbed with oil very frequently'. Celsus also suggested that phthisis required a bland diet with the subsequent addition of elements such as small fish.

Suetonius furnished us with some helpful general information on Augustus' health that might lend some further support to a lung disease hypothesis:

> He also experienced some illnesses which occurred every year at set times; for he would usually feel weak around his birthday [23 September] and he was affected by distension of the stomach [*praecordiorum inflatione*] at the beginning of spring and by a head-cold [*gravedine*] when the wind was from the south. As a consequence, with his body weakened, he could not easily endure either cold or heat'.

The translation of '*praecordiorum inflation*' for 'distension of the stomach' might alternatively be read as 'inflammation/swelling of the diaphragm/midriff'.

Suetonius also added that:

> In the winter he used to protect himself with four tunics and a thick toga, an under-tunic, a woollen chest-protector, and wraps for his thighs and shins; in the summer he would sleep with his bedroom doors open and often in the courtyard with playing water and someone fanning him.

In relation to my hypothesis that Augustus suffered from lung problems, the reference to a woollen chest protector is relevant as is his description of the seasonal and weather-related variations in his symptoms. Modern patients with chronic lung conditions often find their condition is worse at night; opening windows and avoiding indoor air pollutants can help.

Any lung problems would also have been exacerbated by the polluted air in Rome (and inside Roman houses) and, according to Suetonius, 'for more than forty years [Augustus] kept the same bedroom, winter and summer, although he found the city bad for his health in winter and continued to spend the winter there without fail'. Suetonius also mentioned that 'when sick he used to sleep in Maecenas' house'. This property had large gardens, an elevated position and was located in a healthy area according to Horace.

Modern possibilities for Augustus' proposed chronic lung disease include conditions such as asthma, bronchiectasis, chronic obstructive pulmonary disease, pneumonia or tuberculosis. There has been a specific suggestion that Augustus had an atopic tendency with an increased likelihood of asthma. Phthisis has been equated with pulmonary consumption and, subsequently, with modern day tuberculosis. Tuberculosis (TB) was certainly present in Rome at the time of Augustus and modern secondary (re-activated) pulmonary TB has some features in common with Augustus' illness (including symptoms such as fever, weakness, malaise, haemoptysis and pleuritic pain). A primary TB infection might also explain Augustus' illness as a youth.

Malnutrition increases susceptibility to a variety of lung problems including tuberculosis and pneumonia by affecting muscle performance, anatomy and defence mechanisms. It can also lead to slow growth and weight loss alongside symptoms such as tiredness and weakness. Celsus associated *destillatio* with thin or slender individuals. From a young age Augustus was following a prescribed health regimen probably incorporating strict dietary requirements. According to Suetonius: 'as for food he ate very little and for the most part it was ordinary. He was very keen on second-class bread [*secundarium panem*], small fishes, hand-pressed cheeses made from cows' milk, and green figs from the second crop'. He also quoted from one of Augustus' own letters: 'While returning from the Regia by litter, I ate a morsel of bread with a few grapes from a firm-skinned bunch', and commented that, although the Emperor hosted lavish feasts, 'he would sometimes dine alone, either before a dinner party began or after it was over, while touching nothing during the course of the party'. Elsewhere, Suetonius wrote that 'he would arrive at dinner parties late and leave early, as his guests would start eating before he took his place and would continue after he had left'.

It is certainly worth considering if a strict dietary regimen from an early age might have had some effects on Augustus' growth and nutritional status. Suetonius reported that 'he was short of stature', and 'his shoes were elevated a little, so that he would appear taller'. Pliny's description of the episode of oedema at Philippi '*subter cutem fusa turgidi latebra*' could also represent a sign of severe malnutrition.

However, overall, I believe that the evidence assembled is insufficient to allow any greater diagnostic precision in modern medical terminology aside from suggesting that Augustus suffered from a chronic lung disorder. He also lived to 75 and it is argued that such a favourable prognosis was linked to: the relatively infrequent severe lung disease exacerbations (i.e. **EP1**, **EP2** and **EP3**); the absence of any evidence for other serious illnesses (co-morbidities); Augustus' elevated socio-economic position; and following a reasonably healthy lifestyle (aside from the suggested dietary deficiencies).

Diarrhoeal Disease

As discussed earlier, it seems likely that the diarrheal illness that Augustus experienced en route to Nola was significantly downplayed by Suetonius. Moreover, any such problems would have been worsened by the protracted journey, the warm weather, the extremely busy schedule and, according to Velleius, having a 'strong will' that 'resisted infirmity'.

Ensuring that he drank sufficient fresh water onboard a boat for several days might also have been difficult, with the risk that he developed significant dehydration (including symptoms such as weakness [as suggested by Velleius Paterculus] and confusion [as suggested by

Suetonius]). Such a scenario could have been particularly serious given Augustus' advanced age and suggested chronic lung disorder.

There is certainly evidence from paleopathology that diarrhoeal diseases such as dysentery would have present in Italy at the time of Augustus. The impact of such problems would undoubtedly have been exacerbated by the growth of the Empire under Augustus (with improved communications), poor hygiene practices in urban environments and the rapid expansion of city populations. Within Augustan Rome, large numbers of inhabitants would have lived in unsafe and unsanitary conditions, and it has been suggested that Baudel's description of Paris in the sixteenth and seventeenth centuries[19] might equally well be applied to ancient Rome:

> Chamber pots … continued to be emptied out of windows; the streets were sewers. For a long time, Parisians relieved themselves under a row of yews in the Tuileries; driven from here by the Swiss guards, they betook themselves to the banks of the Seine, which was equally revolting to eye and nose.

Historical understanding

Illness and death cast shadows over Augustus' life from an early age. Suetonius commented that 'when he was four he lost his father. When he was eleven he delivered a funeral oration of his late grandmother'. In writing about the *Misfortunes of Augustus*, Pliny commented that 'the deified Augustus … whom men unanimously include in their list of happy individuals, a careful investigator of all the facts would find great changes of human fortune'. He specifically highlighted 'all the mutinies in his armies' alongside 'all his critical illnesses', perhaps to specifically emphasise Augustus' lifelong health challenges.

Although he lived to 75, for over half his life Augustus was preparing for death, even constructing a mausoleum in 28BC. Crook comments that his 'precarious condition, and his own belief in it, must be borne in mind ... it really was possible that the whole story would end abruptly, and he must hasten to leave something stable behind'.[20]

Coming to terms with illness is something that must have both challenged and troubled individuals throughout recorded time. Therefore, it does not seem unreasonable to suggest that Augustus' initial reactions to his illness – and the uncertainty it brought about the future – might have included features akin to modern-day diseases such as anxiety and depression alongside anger. Augustus' brutality and cruelty at Philippi and, also, at Perugia in 41BC may have represented an external manifestation of such anger. Plutarch in his *Sayings of the Romans*, described an intriguing encounter between the philosopher, Athenodorus, and Augustus:

> Athenodorus...because of his advanced years begged to be dismissed and allowed to go home, and Augustus granted his request. ... Athenodorus, as he was taking leave of him, said, 'Whenever you get angry, Caesar, do not say or do anything before repeating to yourself the twenty-four letters of the alphabet'.

However, by the second decade BC, Suetonius paints a picture of an exemplary ruler exhibiting patience, exercising restraint and demonstrating the key Roman virtues of *clementia* (mercy) and *civilitas* (citizen-like behaviour). Augustus even advised the young Tiberius 'not to give in to the emotions of your youth or be too angry'.

David Wardle (2014) comments 'it is clear from the historical record that Augustus' early years were notorious more for the antithesis of *clementia*, namely harshness and cruelty (*severitas* and *crudelitas*)'. It could be that the way he changed over the years was partially about accepting, adapting and adjusting to his chronic lung disorder with the support of his mother and his second wife Livia.

Augustus' coping strategies included taking particular care of his health but also delegating significant authority and responsibility to two individuals – Marcus Agrippa and Gaius Maecenas – for military, architectural, administrative and diplomatic issues. Some specific work adaptations can also be identified in Suetonius:

> He administered justice diligently…if he was unwell from a litter set up on his tribunal or even at home while lying down... he would absent himself from a show for several hours and sometimes for whole days … having appointed others to perform his role as presiding official…he fought two foreign wars by himself, against the Dalmatians…and against the Cantabrians... All the other wars he conducted through legates.

Maybe Augustus and his colleagues sought to reframe his long-term illness in a positive light – as a heroic virtue or a pathway to deification. Also, despite his chronic lung problems and ageing, he was only ever portrayed on statues or coins as being in the prime of life. Image mattered to Augustus and to the Romans a statue was the embodiment of the emperor, sharing some of his power. It is estimated that the original number of such stone or bronze representations of Augustus was between 25,000 and 50,000. Perhaps, this also served to convince Augustus himself that, despite everything, his position remained unassailable.

CHAPTER 6

Tiberius

(42BC–AD37; Emperor from AD14)

The Emperor Tiberius found Augustus a hard act to follow, and, in many ways, his reign was overshadowed by his predecessor's achievements.

Tiberius has been characterised as haughty, arrogant, cruel and perverted but he was also a reclusive and isolated individual. From 22-6BC and again between AD4-10, Tiberius spent the greater part of his time living away from home within army camps in Spain, Armenia, Gaul, Illyricum and Germany. Also, for several years, he 'retired', firstly, to Rhodes (6BC-2AD) and, for his last ten years, lived on Capri. Suetonius wrote that even when he returned to Rome in 2AD 'he at once moved…to the gardens of Maecenas on the Esquiline, where he led a very retired life, merely attending to his personal affairs and exercising no public functions'. After the deaths of his nephew Germanicus and his son Drusus 'he retired to Campania, and almost everyone firmly believed and openly declared that he would never come back'.

Tiberius' father found himself on the wrong side in the civil war, fighting against Augustus, so Tiberius 'passed his infancy and his youth amid hardship and tribulation, since he was everywhere the companion of his parents in their flight'. In 38BC, Augustus took Tiberius' pregnant mother, Livia, as his second wife.

Tiberius' relationships with both his stepfather and his mother must have been challenging. He was not adopted by Augustus as his successor until after the deaths of Marcellus, Gaius Caesar and Lucius Caesar. Even this had strings attached, being required to simultaneously adopt Germanicus as his son and heir ignoring the expectations of Drusus. Moreover, according to Suetonius, 'when Tiberius took his departure, Augustus gasped to his attendants: "Poor Rome, doomed to be masticated by those slow-moving jaws!". I am also aware that... he so disliked Tiberius' dour manner.' Although Livia had worked hard to support and promote Tiberius' interests, their relationship soured over time. When she died, he refused to attend the funeral, forbade her deification and disregarded the provisions of her will.

Healers and Healthcare

While campaigning with Tiberius, the historian Velleius Paterculus witnessed the Emperor's personal involvement with the care of his troops:

> There was not one of us, or of those either above or below our rank, who fell ill without having his health and welfare looked after by Tiberius with as much solicitude indeed as though this were the chief occupation of his mind, preoccupied though he was by his heavy responsibilities. There was a horsed vehicle ready for those who needed it, his own litter was at the disposal of all, and I, among others, have enjoyed its use. Now his physicians, now his kitchen, and now his bathing equipment, brought for this one purpose for himself alone, ministered to the comfort of all who were sick.

On Rhodes, Tiberius spent time visiting the sick and yet he seems to have been particularly wary of doctors.

Plutarch wrote, 'I have heard that Tiberius once said that a man over sixty who holds out his hand to a physician is ridiculous.' And, according to Suetonius, 'he enjoyed excellent health, which was all but perfect during nearly the whole of his reign although from the thirtieth year of his age he took care of it according to his own ideas, without the aid or advice of physicians.' Even when approaching death he rebuked the Imperial physician Charicles for surreptitiously seeking to check his pulse.

Trusting physicians in the ancient world could prove dangerous as some, less reputable doctors, might kill a ruler and pretend the illness or frailty of the patient was simply too severe to counteract. For example, Tiberius' son Drusus died in 23 at the hands of Sejanus (prefect of the Praetorian Guard), Livilla (Drusus' wife) and the physician Eudamus with a poison being chosen that, according to Tacitus, had 'gradual effects resembling ordinary ill-health'. It took eight years – and the torture of Eudamus – for Tiberius to discover the truth that his son had been murdered.

Health Record, Diagnostic Conjectures and Historical Understanding

According to Suetonius, Tiberius was strong, fit and healthy. When his brother Drusus died in 9BC he 'conveyed his body to Rome, going before it on foot all the way'. He did, however, enjoy wine and sometimes overindulged while away on campaigns. Tiberius was also not averse to feigning illness for political purposes in his dealings with Sejanus, Germanicus and the legions.

In terms of specific episodes of illness Augustus did express some concerns in a letter to his adopted son quoted by Suetonius 'when I hear and read that you are worn out by constant hardships … I beseech you to spare yourself, that the news of your illness may not kill your mother and me'. Tiberius was also brought into the senate 'one day when he was sick and carried in a litter'. In addition, the author Aulius Gellius wrote:

> that the citizens of Praeneste earnestly begged the emperor Tiberius that they might be changed from a colony into the condition of a municipium, and that Tiberius granted their request by way of conferring a favour, because in their territory, and near their town itself, he had recovered from a dangerous illness.

A detailed examination of the ancient sources reveals references to a bowel problem, short-sightedness and a skin disorder in addition to highlighting some concerns about Tiberius' mental wellbeing.

Bowel problem (*colum*)

The Latin noun *colum* can be translated as the colon or as a disease of the large intestine (colic). According to Pliny:

> It was in the principate of Tiberius Caesar that this malady made its way into Italy. Nobody suffered from it before the Emperor himself, and the citizens were greatly puzzled when they read in his edict, in which he begged to be excused because of an illness, a name they had never heard before.

Celsus furnished us with a lot more detail about:

> A disease in the larger intestine, which the Greeks call *colum*: When the more lax intestine, which they name *colum*, tends to be painful, and when it is nothing more than an inflation of a sort, the aim should be to promote digestion; to practise reading aloud and other exercises; to use a hot bath, also hot food and drink, and in short, to avoid all manner of cold, all sweets and pulse, and whatever else tends to flatulence.

In a later section, Celsus outlined the sort of symptoms that Tiberius might have experienced. He distinguished the condition from dysentery with bloody diarrhoea:

> There is extreme flatulence, violent pains especially on the right side; the intestine which appears to undergo torsion...almost forces out wind. In most cases it comes on after chills and fits of indigestion, then subsides, and in course of time often recurs so as to be a cause of suffering but without shortening the length of life.

Celsus also indicated that Tiberius' personal physician Cassius had developed a treatment for colic. It consisted of saffron, anise, castory, parsley, pepper both long and round, poppy-tears, round rush, myrrh, nard, all mixed together with honey, which could either be swallowed as it was or dissolved in hot water. Cassius' remedy was carefully recorded by both Scribonius Largus (Claudius' physician) in addition to Galen. Moreover, Pliny included Cassius in a list of the most distinguished court physicians mentioning that his annual salary was 250,000 sesterces.

In modern terms, *colum* could represent a wide range of conditions including gall stones, lead poisoning, inflammatory/infective bowel disease, coeliac disease or food intolerance. Coeliac disease (an immune reaction linked to gluten from wheat, barley or rye) was certainly around in Italy at the time of Tiberius as demonstrated by an isotopic, genetic and morphological examination of the skeletal remains of a young woman from the archaeological site of Cosa in Tuscany.

Pliny mentioned that Tiberius was partial to a plant called *cucumis* 'in fact there was never a day on which he was not supplied with it, as his kitchen-gardeners had beds mounted on wheels which they moved out into the sun and then on wintry days withdrew under the cover of frames glazed with transparent stone'. Traditionally, the Latin noun *cucumis* has been translated as 'cucumber' but could have been any member of the gourd family including melons. What is particularly intriguing is that over-consumption of gourds can result in cucurbitacin intolerance including, perhaps, some of the symptoms exhibited by Tiberius.

Short-sightedness

Eye-related issues were a particular concern in the Roman world, reflecting an ancient view of the eyes as a privileged body part and the transition point between the body and the outside world. Celsus wrote: 'But there are grave and varied mishaps to which our eyes are exposed; and these have so large a part both in the service and the amenity of life, they are to be looked after with the greatest care.' And Pliny the Elder commented:

> Below the forehead are the eyes, which form the most precious portion of the human body, and which, by the enjoyment of the blessings of sight, distinguish life from death ... In all animals there is no part in the whole body that is a stronger exponent of the feelings, and in man more especially, for it is from the expression of the eye that we detect clemency, moderation, compassion, hatred, love, sadness, and joy. From the eyes, too, the various characters of persons are judged of, according as they are ferocious, menacing, sparkling, sedate, leering, askance, downcast, or languishing. Beyond a doubt it is in the eyes that the mind has its abode: sometimes the look is ardent, sometimes fixed and steady, at other times the eyes are humid, and at others, again, half closed. From these it is that the tears of pity flow, and when we kiss them we seem to be touching the very soul.

Based on the ancient sources, the so-called 'bad emperors' such as Nero and Domitian were reported to have weak eyes with poor eyesight and being infamous for their ocular gougings too! According to Tacitus, 'the worst of our torments under Domitian was to see him with his eyes fixed up us.' In relation to Tiberius, Suetonius wrote, 'his eyes were unusually large...had the power of seeing even at night and in the dark, but only for a short time when first opened after sleep; presently they grew dim sighted again' and Pliny explained that 'if he woke up at night for a short time he could see everything just as in bright daylight, although darkness gradually closed over him'. But such descriptions might, at the time, have been understood as indicating a lazy or unjust character rather than anything superhuman!

Cassius Dio suggested that Tiberius had some specific problems with visual acuity: 'At first he kept saying he would give up the rule entirely on account of his age [he was 56] and of his short-sightedness (for although he saw extremely well in the dark, his sight was very poor in the daytime).' As artificial lenses to treat refractive issues, such as Tiberius' possible short-sightedness, were not available to the Romans (but see Chapter 9) Tiberius' only option would have been to try a topical eye preparation from an oculist. Many such eye medicines (*collyria*) were designed to clear the sight (*ad claritatem*) or to treat *caligo*. *Caligo* was poor or blurred vision and, according to Celsus, occurred because of old age or eye inflammation (*lippitudo*...similar to our modern term conjunctivitis). The epitaphs of two eye doctors (*medicus ocularius*) who probably treated Tiberius have also been discovered: Mantias and Thyrius.

A lot of the treatments for eye inflammation were probably quite effective and it is also possible that some preparations might have improved Tiberius' short-sightedness transiently by, perhaps, altering the refractive index of the cornea or constricting the pupil to produce a pinhole effect. Oribasius, physician to the Emperor Julian, certainly recommended that engravers, painters and goldsmiths, if they had trouble with their work, should smear an ointment, prepared from the seeds of pomegranate and honey, on their eyes.

Skin disorder

Tacitus mentioned that Tiberius' face was covered in sores (*ulcerosa*) and plasters (*medicaminibus interstincta*). Suetonius also commented that sometimes numerous swellings (*tumores*) would suddenly break out on his face.

A clue to Tiberius' skin condition can be found in Pliny who wrote about a new disease that had spread to Italy during his reign. He stated that, in many cases it involved 'the whole of the face...covering the skin with a disfiguring scaly eruption' and that 'the nobles were very much affected through the momentary contact of a kiss'. The precise nature of the condition in modern terms is difficult to determine, especially as the treatment being used might have caused additional problems as detailed by Pliny 'the scar left on many who had been hardy enough to endure the treatment was more unsightly than the disease, for caustics were the method employed, and the loathsome complaint broke out afresh unless the flesh was burnt through right to the bones'.

It seems most likely that the skin problem that had arisen in Rome (and may have affected Tiberius) was due to either a bacterial or a viral infection. In modern terms, one possible candidate is herpes simplex that can easily be spread by close contact, including kissing. It is also intriguing to note that, according to Suetonius, Tiberius issued an edict forbidding social kissing.

Tiberius' appearance must have been well-remembered as, over the years, his skin condition acquired a legendary status linked to the rise of Christianity. In the sixth-century text *Cura sanitates Tiberii* he was described as being gravely ill with ulcers and fevers but, once he had viewed an image of Jesus imprinted on a cloth (the Veronica), he was cured.

Mental wellbeing

Pliny described Tiberius as the 'saddest of men' and he was perceived as gloomy by Augustus too. According to Suetonius:

> He strode along with his neck stiff and bent forward, usually with a stern countenance and for the most part in silence, never or rarely conversing with his companions, and then speaking with great deliberation…his anxious/troubled mind (*anxiam mentem*) became torture because of reproaches of all kinds from every quarter…in utter self-disgust he all but admitted the extremity of his wretchedness in a letter…'may all the gods and goddesses visit me with more utter destruction than I feel that I am daily suffering'.

Over the years, his relationships with family members and friends also deteriorated – 'he had a father's affection for neither his own son Drusus nor his adopted son Germanicus…even when [Drusus] died, Tiberius was not greatly affected.' Suetonius wrote that, from

25 onwards 'he broke out into every form of cruelty...venting it on his...mother, then on his grandsons and daughter-in-law, and finally on Sejanus'. It is also suspected that he was indirectly involved in the poisoning of Germanicus too.

One specific episode does suggest that Tiberius might have experienced bouts of *tristitia* (probably similar to modern-day depression – see Chapter 7) aside from just being sad. For around nine years, Tiberius was very happily married to Vipsania Agrippina and they had a son, Drusus. But when Vipsania was expecting their second child in 11BC, Tiberius was instructed by the Emperor to divorce her and to marry Julia, Augustus' somewhat wayward daughter. According to Suetonius, the event caused Tiberius great mental anguish (*non sine magno angore animi*) and, subsequently, when 'he accidently caught sight of Vipsania and followed her with tears in his eyes and intense unhappiness written on his face, precautions were taken against his ever seeing her again'.

Over the next few years, Tiberius spent most of his time away from home in Germany or the Balkans and during this period, aside from a difficult marriage, he had to cope with the death of his brother, Drusus the Elder. In 6BC, at the age of 36, 'though in the prime of life, in excellent health...Tiberius decided to retire as completely as possible from state affairs'. He did not return to Rome for seven years and various elements of the story detailed by Suetonius suggest that the episode had many features similar to modern-day depression.

'He asked for leave of absence on the ground of weariness of office and a desire to rest'. This suggests that he lacked energy and perhaps his sleep was disturbed too.

'When efforts were made to detain him, he refused to take food for four days.' This suggests some intention to harm himself.

'He left his wife and son in Rome and went down to Ostia in haste, without saying a single word to any who saw him off, and kissing only a very few when he left.' This suggests that he was becoming more socially withdrawn.

In seeking to explain the reasons behind Tiberius' self-imposed exile on Rhodes, Suetonius highlighted Tiberius' difficult relationship with Julia in addition to possible low self-esteem linked to his deteriorating position in the hierarchy of succession at the time (behind Augustus' grandsons).

On Rhodes, he lived modestly and 'also gave up his usual exercises with horses and arms, and laying aside the garb of his country, wore a Greek coat and slippers'. For a troubled individual seeking some peace and quiet, Rhodes was a perfect choice; Tiberius had been there about fifteen years before and 'had cherished pleasant memories of that beautiful and healthy island'. Over the years, Tiberius had also developed an interest in Hellenism and learnt about Stoicism from the Greco-Egyptian scholar and astrologer Thrasyllus, who became a member of his household in Rhodes. Intriguingly, the island was a centre for Stoic philosophy during the first century BC and Posidonius of Rhodes is reported to have introduced Stoicism into the Roman world. Perhaps Tiberius was searching for a philosophy of life and tranquillity to overcome his sadness, depression and anxiety.

It may have been a desire for a similar setting to Rhodes that subsequently drove him to the Villa Jovis on Capri in 26 for his second period of exile from Rome. This time, according to Suetonius:

> he utterly neglected the conduct of state affairs, from that time on never filling the vacancies in the decuries of the knights, nor changing the tribunes of the soldiers and prefects or the governors of any of the provinces. He left Spain and Syria without consular governors for several years, suffered Armenia to be overrun by the Parthians, Moesia to be laid waste by the Dacians and Sarmatians, and the Gallic provinces by the Germans, to the great dishonour of the empire and no less to its danger.

Aside from possible depression/anxiety, Tiberius has been labelled as having a range of other modern psychiatric conditions including obsessive-compulsive personality disorder and severe paranoia. However, it is important to tread extremely carefully in generating such diagnoses as the boundaries of mental illness are socially constructed and highly culturally dependent.

In reflecting on Tiberius' character, Tacitus remarked on the nobility and fame he achieved 'while he lived as a great official under Augustus' but how 'when the restraints of shame and fear were gone, and nothing remained but to follow his own bent, he plunged impartially into crime and into ignominy'. Lucius Arruntius wondered 'if Tiberius, in spite of all his experience, has been transformed and deranged by absolute power, will Caligula, barely out of his boyhood, ignorant of all things and nurtured amid the worst, do better?' This is a question that will be explored further in Chapter 7.

Death

The exact cause of Tiberius' death is open to debate. He might have succumbed to a natural death but there are also suggestions that he was poisoned, suffocated using a pillow, strangled by Caligula or deprived of food. By carefully examining the ancient sources it is possible to tease out four main phases in his death that, taken together, suggest a more natural end to Tiberius' passing aged 77 years.

Phase 1

According to Suetonius, 'twice only during the whole period of his retirement did he try to return to Rome' and, on the second occasion he was within 11 kilometres of the city when 'he went back in haste to Campania, fell ill at Astura, but recovering somewhat kept on to Circeii'. The journey he made back to Astura was probably around 62km with a further 40km being covered to reach Circeii.

Phase 2

At Circeii 'to avoid giving any suspicion of his weak condition, he not only attended the games...but even threw down darts from his high seat at a board …in the arena. Immediately he was taken with a pain in the side…and his illness increased.'

Phase 3

Tiberius then travelled around 134km to Misenum and:

> made no change to his usual habits, not even giving up his banquets and other pleasures, partly from lack of self-denial and partly to conceal his condition. Indeed, when the physician Charicles had taken his hand to kiss it as he left the dining room, since he was going away on leave of absence, Tiberius, thinking that he was trying to feel his pulse, urged him to remain and take his place again.

According to Tacitus:

> There was a doctor of repute...Charicles, who had been accustomed not to treat the illnesses of the emperor but to offer him opportunities for consulting him. While taking his departure on the plea of private business, he clasped the Caesar's hand, apparently as an act of respect, and felt the pulse. The device was detected. Tiberius – possibly offended, and therefore making a special effort to conceal his anger – ordered the dinner to proceed… Still, Charicles assured Macro that Tiberius' respiration was failing.

Phase 4

Cassius Dio covered Tiberius' final hours in the context of his general health as follows:

> He died at Misenum… He had been ill for a good while, but expected to live because of…a prophecy, he neither consulted

> his physicians nor changed his manner of life; and so, wasting away gradually, as he was well stricken in years and subject to a sickness that was not severe, he would often all but expire and then recover again… Caligula, therefore, fearing that his health might actually be restored, refused his requests for something to eat, on the ground that it would hurt him, and pretending that he needed warmth, wrapped him up in many thick clothes and so smothered him.

Tacitus' description is similar in that Tiberius appeared to have stopped breathing and died but then 'word came that he was recovering his speech and sight and calling for someone to bring him food as a restorative after his funny turn'.

Suetonius outlined Tiberius' last moments:

> Some say that a pillow was thrown upon his face, when he came to and asked for a ring that had been taken from him during a fainting fit. Seneca writes that conscious of his approaching end he took off the ring, as if to give it to someone, but held fast to it for a time; then put it back on his finger, and clenching his left hand, lay for a long time motionless; suddenly he called for his attendants, and on receiving no response, got up; but his strength failed him and he fell dead near the couch.

In summary it seems that, in the context of a long and psychologically stressful journey, the elderly Tiberius became unwell, experienced pain in his side after exercise and then deteriorated further. His physician clearly felt it was important to check his pulse and noted that his respiration was affected too. Tiberius also suffered from episodes of loss of consciousness before a final catastrophic collapse. In modern terms, the story is suggestive of death due a major cardiovascular event such as a heart attack, an aortic dissection or a pulmonary embolism.

CHAPTER 7

Caligula

(12–41; Emperor from 37)

Caligula was the son of Germanicus and Agrippina the Elder as well as the grandson of Tiberius' brother Drusus the Elder. Although he was given the name Gaius Caesar Augustus Germanicus at birth, he is often referred to as 'Caligula' linked to the small military boots be wore as a child. In this chapter, the name Caligula will be used throughout.

Caligula's childhood and teenage years were challenging. Having accompanied his father to Syria in 17, Germanicus was allegedly poisoned and died at the age of 33. Tacitus painted a particularly poignant image of the 7-year-old Caligula's return to the shores of Italy: 'when Agrippina together with her two children stepped from the ship holding the funeral urn…a concerted groan arose from the whole gathering' adding that the funeral party itself was 'exhausted from protracted grief'.

Back in Rome, Caligula lived with his mother, brothers and sisters but in 27, Agrippina the Elder was put under house arrest and exiled. He then moved in with his great-grandmother Livia and, when she died, his grandmother Antonia Minor. Two years later, at the age of 19, he was summoned to Capri by his great uncle (and adoptive grandfather) Tiberius. Caligula must have been aware of his precarious position given the Emperor's treatment of his two older brothers, Nero Julius Caesar and Drusus Caesar. According to Suetonius: 'both were declared public enemies… They think that Nero was forced into suicide when an executioner, purportedly sent on senatorial authority, showed him the noose and hooks, while Drusus was so deprived of food that he tried to eat the stuffing from his mattress'. Agrippina the Elder died in 33 and, according to Tacitus, 'she took her own life – unless perhaps she was refused food to produce a death that could be taken for suicide'.

Although Tiberius' son Drusus had died in 23, he still had a grandson, Tiberius Gemellus. Caligula, as the adopted grandson, would have had to tread extremely carefully in his dealings with the Princeps and, moreover, keep tight control on his reactions to events. Tacitus wrote that he 'concealed a monstrous personality beneath a deceitful veneer of moderation and uttered not a word at his mother's condemnation or his brother's ruin. Whatever Tiberius' mood for the day seemed to be he would adopt the same, using language little different from his.'

All these experiences must have taken an enormous toll on the psychological wellbeing of the young Caligula. Perhaps some of the stories concerning his behaviour on Capri are external manifestations of internal mental turmoil with Suetonius writing 'his cruel and wayward nature he could not even then supress to the point of taking very keen interest in punishments and penalties of those surrendered for torture; and hidden under a wig and long robe he would prowl around at night on gluttonous and lecherous escapades'.

Tiberius demonstrated some warmth to Caligula on his arrival in Capri praising his '*pietas*' and '*indoles*' (sense of duty and good character). He also, according to Cassius Dio, 'gave some indications that he intended to make him successor to the throne.' But later, the Emperor commented that he was 'nurturing a viper for the Roman people.' Also, according to Philo of Alexandria, he 'doubted his fitness for an office of such magnitude, both because of his unsociable and unfriendly nature and also because of his erratic temperament, for he showed abnormal and crazy tendencies and maintained no consistency in word and deed.'

Although it has been suggested that Caligula eventually poisoned, starved or smothered his predecessor, he appears to have commenced his reign on a positive note. He showed great deference to the senate, suspended charges under Tiberius' controversial law of '*maiestas*' (loosely 'treason') and permitted much greater freedom of expression.

Cassius Dio wrote, 'he published, as Augustus had done, all the accounts of the public funds… He helped the soldiers to extinguish a conflagration and rendered assistance to those who suffered loss by it'. To the Romans, virtues represented characteristics that individuals were expected to exhibit, and '*pietas*' was particularly important being about duty, respect and family loyalty. On assuming the purple, Caligula certainly demonstrated *pietas* by, for example, travelling to the islands of Pontia and Pandateria to retrieve the ashes of his mother and brothers. Coins were struck honouring his dead family members and it was reported that he was kind and generous to his adopted brother Tiberius Gemellus too.

However, after a honeymoon period of less than a year, Caligula's behaviour seemed to change. The writers Suetonius and Cassius Dio characterised him as a narcissistic megalomaniac who was sexually depraved, sadistic and profligate with a taste for the theatrical and the bizarre. He was described as practicing incest with his sisters, participating in orgies, and forcing sexual intercourse on the wives of his rivals. Allegedly he took pleasure in physically torturing his victims too, even killing a senator simply because he had become the centre of attention to the detriment of Caligula. He also adopted what were considered inappropriate disguises during public events, wearing clothing overloaded with precious stones and impersonating several gods and goddesses including Jupiter, Neptune, Apollo and Venus. He enthusiastically participated in chariot races and plays alongside coachmen and professional actors.

Although Caligula only ruled for four years, few other Roman emperors surpass his reputation for infamy. To account for this, it has been suggested that he suffered from a variety of physical and mental conditions.

Healers and Healthcare

There is little information available on healers during Caligula's brief reign but it seems likely that some individuals, such as C. Stertinius

Xenophon, who subsequently served Claudius had looked after Caligula. However, Josephus commented on the laudable actions of one doctor, Alcyon, immediately following Caligula's assassination as he had exited the theatre. Within minutes the Imperial German bodyguards:

> with drawn swords surrounded the theatre, [and] the audience all expected to die…there was no escape… It was Alcyon the doctor who was responsible for their welcome release. When he was seized to look after the wounded, he sent out those who were with him – supposedly to fetch the materials needed for his treatment of the casualties, but in fact to get away from the danger they were in.

Health Record, Diagnostic Conjectures and Historical Understanding

In considering the health record of Caligula two specific illness episodes can be discerned from the available literature. There is also a more general question about his mental health.

Specific illness episodes

Prior to 20

Suetonius wrote that, as a boy, Caligula 'was troubled by the falling sickness (*comitiali morbo*), and while in his youth he had some endurance, yet at times because of sudden faintness (*defection*) he was hardly able to walk, to stand up, to collect his thoughts, or to hold himself upright'. Celsus described the clinical features of *comitialis morbus* as follows: 'the man suddenly falls down and foam issues out of his mouth; after an interval he returns to himself, and actually gets up by himself... And usually it persists even until the day of death without danger to life.' The only other possible allusion to any concerns about Caligula's early health is contained within a letter from Augustus quoted by Suetonius concerning a journey to be undertaken by the

2-year-old boy: 'I made arrangements to bring your son to you… I am also sending with him one of my slaves, a doctor.'

Considering the information provided by Suetonius alongside Celsus it seems possible that the young Caligula might have suffered from a condition not unlike epilepsy. More specifically it has been argued that Caligula could have been affected by temporal lobe or petit mal epilepsy with the former condition accounting for his later behaviour as Princeps. Also, although there are no reports of Caligula suffering from fits as an adult, it has been suggested that he subsequently developed 'fit phobia'. But it is important to appreciate that, even today, differentiating a fainting episode from an epileptic seizure can sometimes be quite tricky based simply on the symptoms reported by a patient. Interrogating those who might have witnessed an episode is critical and it is important to be cautious about relying on second-hand information. Suetonius never met Caligula and was writing about the events of the Emperor's reign around eighty years after he had died. Also, contemporary sources such as Philo and Seneca didn't make any reference to Caligula suffering from anything approaching a fit or a faint. It is also possible that Caligula's supporters might have been seeking to associate him, at least in his early years, with a condition that had affected his eminent great-grandfather Julius Caesar. According to Suetonius, Julius Caesar also suffered from *comitialis morbus*.

37–38

Philo of Alexandria wrote, 'In the eighth month Caligula was struck down by severe sickness.' He probably fell ill sometime after 18 October 37 with epigraphic evidence suggesting that he was still out of action the following January.[21] This illness is also reported by Suetonius and Cassius Dio suggesting that it was a significant historical event. Moreover, according to Philo, 'The news of Caligula's illness travelled everywhere…so people…became dismal. Every household and city was filled with anxiety and dejection, their recent joy being counter-balanced by a grief no less intense.' And when he recovered, 'the good news of his complete recovery...every continent, every island, returned once more to its former happiness.'

It has been argued that this severe illness could have inflicted permanent damage on Caligula, leading to changes in his behaviour and actions. Perhaps he had suffered from a brain injury due to a type of encephalitis, prolonged epileptic seizures (status epilepticus), the excessive consumption of lead or alcohol, or even developed acute thyrotoxicosis (an overactive thyroid gland). But the evidence in support of most of these suggestions is, at best, tenuous. Moreover, Caligula's reasoning, understanding and intelligence seems to have been unaffected, with Tacitus commenting that 'even Caligula's disturbed mind did not spoil the power of his speaking'. The idea of epilepsy-related brain damage also presupposes that Caligula suffered from epilepsy in the first instance which, as discussed earlier, remains uncertain. Philo mentioned Caligula's 'hard drinking' and, due to the addition of lead-containing *sapa* to Roman wines to improve the taste, there might also have been a correlation between alcohol consumption and lead poisoning. However, there is absolutely no clinical information available to support either diagnosis.

In the 1970s, the physician Robert Katz[22] amalgamated the various references to restlessness, insomnia, hyperactivity and increased appetite together with a physical description of Caligula and diagnosed thyrotoxicosis. Suetonius had certainly written that 'Insomnia was his worst torment. Three hours a night of fitful sleep were all that he ever got' and that 'he moved about excitedly while speaking'. Philo had also commented that Caligula's appetite was 'still unsatisfied when the cavities were stuffed full' and, in appearance, Caligula was described as very tall, nearly bald with a pallid complexion, a very thin neck, unshapely body and spindly legs. However, extreme caution must be exercised in using vague and non-specific symptoms to make precise diagnoses within any historical period. Moreover, such symptoms are context-dependent and, on occasions, can even serve as metaphors for the virtues or the vices of an emperor. To the Romans, an individual's outward appearance was also considered key to their character, so, although hair loss might suggest a thyroid disorder to a modern physician, the ancient authors could have magnified its significance for good or for bad. The reported discordance between Caligula's features – tall but unshapely – perhaps allowed Suetonius to mirror his purported moral grotesqueness by his physical grotesqueness too. A further level of complexity is that the surviving stone busts of Caligula depict a good-looking man seemingly remote from the Suetonius' later description.

Thus, although there seems little doubt that Caligula was significantly ill during this period, the precise nature of the illness remains elusive in modern terms. It also seems doubtful that this illness was the immediate cause of the reported changes in Caligula's behaviours and actions. Although the start of the illness can be dated to 37, his serious excesses and clashes with the senate seem only to have commenced around eighteen months later. But perhaps the sickness focused Caligula's attention on the precarious nature of his position and his tenuous hold on power. More specifically, he would have witnessed how close colleagues, such as his adopted brother Tiberius Gemellus, responded to his incapacity. Cassius Dio wrote:

> After this he fell sick, but instead of dying himself he caused the death of Tiberius [Gemellus]… The complaint made against the lad was that he had prayed and expected that Caligula would die; and he destroyed many others too, on this same charge. So Tiberius [Gemellus] perished on suspicion of having been watching his chance to profit from the Emperor's illness. On the other hand, Publius Afranius Potitus, a plebeian, perished, because in a burst of foolhardy servility he had promised not only of his own free will but also under oath that he would give his life if only Gaius should recover.

Two other significant life events occurred around the same time as Caligula's illness: the death of his first wife, Junia Claudilla, during childbirth as well as the passing of his favourite sister Drusilla. According to Suetonius, Drusilla had been made Caligula's heir and he reacted badly when she died in June 38:

> At her death he made it a capital offence to laugh, to bathe, or to dine with one's parents, wives, or children while the period of public mourning lasted; and was so grazed with grief that he suddenly rushed from Rome by night, drove through Campania, took ship to Sicily, and returned just as impetuously without having shaved or cut his hair in the meantime.

Caligula's close relationship with all his sisters is also demonstrated by the issue of coins between 37 and 38 mentioning all three by name. Accusations of incest between Caligula and his sisters were possibly fuelled by the fact that they played the sort of public ceremonial role normally reserved for a wife.

Mental health

Suetonius wrote that Caligula:

> was sick both physically and mentally (*animi*)… He was well aware he had mental trouble (*mentis valitudinem*), and sometimes proposed taking a leave of absence from Rome to clear his brain; Caesonia [his fourth wife] is reputed to have given him an aphrodisiac which drove him mad (*furorem*). Insomnia was his worst torment… I am convinced that this brain-sickness accounted for his two contradictory vices – over-confidence and extreme timorousness.

Tacitus, also relying on secondary sources, described Caligula as having a disordered mind '*turbidus animi*' in addition to a disturbed mind '*turbata mens*'.

Based on the information contained within the ancient literature several modern authors have retrospectively diagnosed Caligula as suffering from a severe mental illness such as schizophrenia, bipolar disorder, major depression/anxiety or a personality disorder. The term *Caesarenwahnsinn* was also coined to characterise the pathological arrogance associated with unlimited authority. For some individuals it has been suggested that unrestrained power magnifies any pre-existing negative psychological characteristics. The essential elements of *Caesarenwahnsinn* are ostentation, cruelty, theatricality and self-aggrandisement to the point of belief in one's own divinity.

In 1894, the German politician and pacifist Ludwig Quidde applied the diagnosis of *Caesarenwahnsinn* to Caligula echoing Josephus' comment: 'In this first and second year Caligula… promoted much good will for himself… Afterwards, however, because of the extent of this power left the point of thinking as a human'.[23] Quidde particularly highlighted Caligula's pomp, extravagance, waste and cruelty alongside his craving for military triumphs and obsessive interests in drama. He also commented that '*Caesarenwahnsinn* is the product of conditions that can only flourish in the moral degeneration of monarchically-minded peoples or at least of the higher classes which made up the ruler's immediate environment.'

Many contemporary readers of Quidde's seventeen-page pamphlet saw similarities between Caligula's purported megalomania, madness, vanity and ruthless use of power and the activities of Kaiser Wilhelm II and his government. Unfortunately for Quidde, his historical and psychological narrative of an unpredictable emperor whose reign was marked by decline and decadence came to be widely re-interpreted as a thinly veiled critique of political life within Wilhelmine Germany. He narrowly managed to avoid conviction and incarceration by denying the charges and putting the prosecution in the embarrassing position of insisting on the similarities. For example, Wilhelm had once signed his own photograph for an admirer with one of Caligula's favourite quotes '*oderint dum metuant*' ('let them hate, as long as they fear'). The incident nevertheless effectively ended Quidde's research career and he was subsequently imprisoned for three months on a separate charge.

But in considering the application of any 'modern' psychiatric diagnoses, there is a requirement to be particularly wary of the biases and distortions within the ancient sources when dealing with the broad concept of 'madness'. A variety of Latin nouns such as '*insania*' (insanity) or '*furor*' (mad/raving/fury) were harnessed to discredit socially undesirable behaviour. For example, in addition to '*furor*' Tacitus used '*vaecordia*' (folly/madness) and '*rabies*' (madness/frenzy) in describing the mutiny of Germanicus' Legions. Pliny adopted the term '*regum insaniam*' when commenting about rulers' excessive expenditures on building schemes.

It is also possible that Caligula might have been defamed after his death by means of a 'madness narrative' linked to his supposed rejection of the norms of Roman society, his purported challenge to divine authority and his apparently unrestrained, irrational behaviour. Within the works of Suetonius and Cassius Dio the recurrent emphasis on Caligula's vices of '*superbia*' (pride/arrogance), '*saevitia*' (cruelty) and '*aviritia*' (greed) need to be considered in relation to the traditional Roman virtues of '*clementia*' (mercy), '*pietas*' (duty/respect), '*dignitas*' (dignity), '*veritas*' (truthfulness) and '*frugalitas*' (frugality).

Perhaps developing a 'madness narrative' also helped the ancient authors to understand and explain a significant period of change during the first century AD with the tricky transition from Roman Republic to Principate. Sittig[24] suggests that labelling a leader as 'mad' highlights the ongoing political and social upheavals during this time with divergent interpretations of social practices, virtues and vices. By branding some of the actions of Caligula as 'mad', the ancient authors were also, perhaps, promoting their own views about proper Imperial behaviour in the context of a Republican value system as opposed to the (developing) monarchical system. A posthumous diagnosis of madness is a useful mechanism for an emperor to distance himself from a predecessor too, allowing new laws to be enacted, old laws to be rescinded or to simply abrogate any responsibility for murder or other serious crimes.

More generally it is important to appreciate that the boundaries of mental illness are socially constructed and culturally dependent. In considering references to possible mental illness in the ancient literature, distinctions need to be drawn between specialist (medical and legal) and non-specialist authors. A comment in the *SHA* demonstrates the specialist use of the Latin word '*furiosus*' (mad/raving/furious): 'one of the slaves of the household rushed at him [Hadrian] *furiosius* with a sword… Afterwards, when it was found that the man was *furiosum*, he turned him over to the physicians for treatment.' The writings of Celsus (c. 30-40) represent the first specialist medical Roman source to consider the disease '*insania*' (insanity). He also described four varieties of '*insania*'.

Phrenesis from the Greek φρένησιν (madness, delirium, frenzy) 'during the paroxysm of a fever, patients are delirious and talk nonsense'. It can be of 'short duration…does not require any other remedy than that prescribed for the curing of the fever'.

Phrenesis cum continua dementia (being out of one's mind with madness on a continuing basis):

> The mind becomes at the mercy of imaginings…some persons are *tristes* (sad/gloomy), others *hilares* (cheerful/merry); some are more readily controlled and rave in words only, others are rebellious and act with violence; and of these latter, some only do harm by impulse, others are artful too, and show the most complete appearance of sanity whilst seizing occasion for mischief.
>
> In dealing with patients suffering from this type of insanity it is necessary to proceed according to the nature of each case… Some need to have empty fears relieved. Others need to have their violence restrained… In some untimely laughter has to be

Above: **Plate 1.** Seawater bath Sliema, Malta.

Right: **Plate 2.** Image from the *Scrivias* manuscript.

Above: **Plate 21.** Mosaic depicting a theatrical mask in the form of a woman's head (first century AD). Rabat, Malta.

Left: **Plate 22.** Bust of a youthful Marcus Aurelius (Uffizi Gallery).

> put a stop to…in others *tristes* thoughts are to be dissipated… More often, however, the patient is to be agreed with rather than opposed, and his mind slowly and imperceptibly to be turned from the irrational talk to something better. At times also his interest should be awakened; as may be done in the case of men fond of literature… But certainly for all so affected sleep is both difficult and especially necessary.

Tristitia (sad/gloomy): 'of longer duration…caused by black bile'. 'Blood-letting is here of service…and white hellebore…the motions are to be kept very soft, causes of fright excluded, good hope rather put forward; entertainment sought by storytelling and by games.'

Insania longissimum (prolonged insanity):

> This type of insanity is of all the most prolonged whilst it does not shorten life, for usually the patient is robust…we must note in the first place whether the patients are *tristes* or *hilares*…the illness is less serious when accompanied by laughter.
>
> For *tristes* black hellebore should be given as a purge, for *hilares* white hellebore as an emetic…they should not be left alone… they ought to have a change of scene.

Only two individuals who wrote about Caligula ever had any direct contact with the emperor: Seneca the Younger and Philo of Alexandria. Seneca had his literary style derided by Caligula and was very nearly put to death, Philo, as a Jew, viewed him as an enemy of his people. But, although both individuals would undoubtably not have been great fans of Caligula, their comments provide a unique contemporary insight into his mental health.

Nine of Seneca's *Dialogues* mentioned Caligula, and he appeared at the end of *Apocolocyntosis* too, demanding Claudius as his slave.

In six of them, and as such the most repeated element of Seneca's characterisation, is the idea of 'madness'. Seneca used a variety of words to suggest that Caligula was mentally unwell including '*dementia*' (being out of one's mind), '*insania*' (insanity), '*furor*' (mad/raving/fury), '*conturbatus*' (confused/disturbed) and '*intemperies animi*' (stormy mind). Although Seneca might not have intended to make a clinical diagnosis, being rhetorical rather than scientific, it is intriguing that he makes use of Celsus' terms '*insania*' and '*dementia*'. Moreover, in a different context Seneca demonstrated familiarity with the word '*phrensin*', although he does not apply it specifically to Caligula: '*phrensin* and *insanium* are essential to strength, since *furor* often makes men more powerful.'

Philo had led a delegation of Alexandrian Jews to Rome in 40 and met with Caligula for a prolonged period. The previous year they had only had a brief encounter:

> After first greeting us in the plain by the Tiber, as he issued from the gardens left him by his mother, he repeated his salutation and waved his right hand signifying good will and…with the message 'I will hear your statement of case myself when I get a good opportunity'. Consequently everyone…rejoiced…as though we had already won the case…but...what gave joy to others rather alarmed me. Actually he was our mortal foe, beguiling us with the seeming geniality with which he eyed us and the increased cheeriness of his address.

In some extracts from *The Embassy to Gaius*, Philo paints a fascinating picture of the second and much longer meeting in the gardens and villas belonging to Maecenas and Lamia:

> It is right that I should record also both what we saw and what we heard when we were summoned to take a part in the contention about our citizenship. The moment we entered we knew from

his look and movements that we had come into the presence not of a judge but an accuser.

The actual proceedings showed a ruthless tyrant with a menacing frown on his despotic brow. Instead of doing anything…he sent for the two stewards of the two gardens…in which he had been spending three or four days… He ordered them to leave the villas completely open as he wished to make a careful survey of each of them.

When we were brought into his presence…we bowed our heads to the ground with all respect and timidity and saluted him… The mildness and kindness with which he replied to our greeting was such that we gave up not only our case but our lives for lost! In a sneering, snarling way he said 'Are you the god-haters who do not believe me to be a god, a god acknowledged among all the other nations but not to be named by you?'...the envoys on the other side…danced about and invoked blessings… he was delighted at being addressed as of more than human nature. We cried out...'we did sacrifice…the first time on your accession to the sovereignty, the second when you escaped the severe sickness…the third…for victory in Germany.' 'All right' he replied, 'that is true...but...you have not sacrificed to me.'

While he was saying this he was going on with his survey of the houses…some he censured as defective in structure, and for others he made his own plans and gave orders that they should be magnificent. Then driven along we followed him up and down mocked and reviled by our adversaries, as they do in mimes at the theatre. But after giving some of his orders about the buildings he [asked] 'Why do you refuse to eat pork?' The question was greeted by an outburst of laughter from some of our opponents… The laughter was so great that some…were annoyed at it as showing disrespect for the emperor, with whom even a tempered smile is unsafe. We answered, 'Different people have different customs and the use of such things is forbidden to us'…

> whereupon Caligula laughed and said, 'Quite right too, for it's not nice'. Under such befooling and reviling we were helpless.
>
> Then tardily going on a different tack he said, 'We want to hear what claims you make about your citizenship.' We started to speak and give him the information, but when he had had a taste of our pleading…he dashed at high speed into the large room of the house, and walked round it and ordered the windows all round to be restored with transparent stones.
>
> Then he advanced in a leisurely way and said in a more moderate tone, 'What is it that you say?' and when we began on the points which came next in the thread of our argument he ran again into another room and ordered original pictures to be put up there. So with the statement of our case thus mangled and disjointed, one may almost say cut short and crushed to pieces, we gave up, for there was no strength left in us, and since we all the time expected nothing else but death. And God taking compassion on us he relaxed into a softer mood and just said this, 'They seem to me to be people unfortunate rather than wicked and to be foolish in refusing to believe that I have got the nature of a god,' and saying this he went off bidding us to be gone also.

Reading this passage from the perspective of a twenty-first century doctor I might wonder if Caligula's haughtiness, bloated self-image, attention-seeking and impulsive behaviour, disregard for the views of others, arrogance, mischievousness and abrupt emotional outbursts characterise an individual with some type of personality disorder. He also seemed to relish playing an eccentric showman with a bizarre and malevolent sense of humour. There are certainly other examples within the ancient literature of his dark humour, including the following from Suetonius:

> When the bridge across the sea at Puteoli was being blessed, he invited a number of spectators from the shore to inspect it; then

> abruptly tipped them into the water. Some clung to the ships' rudders, but he had them dislodged with boat hooks and oars, and left to drown.

There seems little doubt that Caligula was no fool. Although, like Philo, Josephus viewed Caligula as the enemy of the Jewish people he commented that he was a 'first rate orator, well trained in both Greek and Latin; replying off the cuff to other people's elaborate and long-prepared speeches, even on the weightiest subjects...This was the result of a natural facility.' Suetonius also mentioned his oratorical skills in addition to his views on the works of others such as Virgil and Livy. A well-educated Roman such as Caligula would have had some understanding of a wide range of topics including medicine and, intriguingly, one of his quips, reported by Suetonius, revealed a significant insight into the contemporary treatment of *tristitia* and *insania longissimum*: 'One ex-praetor, taking a mental cure at Anticyra, made frequent requests for extension of his sick leave; Caligula had his throat cut, suggesting that if hellebore had been of so little benefit over so long a period, he must need to be bled.'

As mentioned earlier, Suetonius also suggested that Caligula had insight into his mental state and was particularly troubled by insomnia (as occurs in *phrenesis cum continua dementia*). Moreover, if he had been familiar with the prevailing medical treatments for *insania*, some of his actions such as 'taking a leave of absence from Rome to clear his brain' alongside his passionate interests in literature and theatre could even be viewed as a rational desire to care for his own disordered mental health.

Death

The description of the events surrounding Caligula's death differs between the reports by Josephus and Suetonius with the latter providing much more detail:

> Chaerea came up behind, and gave him a deep cut on his neck, having first cried, 'Take that'...Sabinus...stabbed him in the breast...and as Caligula looked up he split his jawbone with a blow of his sword. As he lay upon the ground and with writhing limbs called out that he still lived, the others dispatched him with thirty wounds...some even thrust their swords through his privates.

The gruesome and violent details provided by Suetonius demonstrate his perspective on Caligula as an example of a 'bad emperor'. It has even been suggested that Caligula's death was deliberately framed as a commentary on his life: a tyrant humbled, an executioner executed, and a would-be usurper of divinity exposed as a mere mortal.[25]

CHAPTER 8

Claudius

(10BC–AD54, Emperor from AD41)

Claudius did not become emperor until the age of 50, but his subsequent fourteen-year reign was marked by some significant achievements. For example, improving the food security for the citizens of Rome (by draining the Fucine lake and constructing a harbour at Ostia) and completing several major civil engineering projects including aqueducts and roads. Claudius also took a keen personal interest in public administration, justice and finance.

However, during the reigns of his three imperial predecessors he had lived largely in the shadows with very limited power or influence. According to Suetonius, 'throughout almost the whole course of his childhood and youth he suffered so severely from various obstinate disorders that the vigour of both his mind and his body was dulled, and even when he reached the proper age, he was not thought capable of any public or private business.'

Suetonius related that Claudius' mother, Antonia, called him 'a monster of a man, not finished but merely begun', and his grandmother either ignored him or treated him with utmost contempt. Even his sister Livilla prayed that he would never become emperor and that 'the Roman people might be spared so cruel and undeserved a fortune'. Measures were also taken to limit Claudius' public visibility: Augustus forbade him from occupying the imperial box at the circus games, he wore a cloak to cover himself at the gladiatorial games and, on occasions, was transported around Rome at night within an enclosed litter.

To Augustus, Claudius was somewhat of an enigma, with Suetonius quoting from a letter he wrote to Livia:

> We must decide once for all what plan we are to adopt in his case. For if he be sound and so to say complete, what reason have we for doubting that he ought to be advanced through the same grades and steps through which his brother [Germanicus] has been advanced?...the poor fellow is unlucky; for in important matters, where his mind does not wander, the nobility of his character is apparent enough.

The only public office that Claudius held during the principate of Augustus was that of priest and he didn't become Consul for the first time until 37. In the meantime, Suetonius tells us, he 'abandoned all hope of advancement and gave himself up to idleness, living in obscurity, he incurred the reproach of drunkenness and gambling, in addition to his former reputation for dullness'.

Claudius married four times producing five offspring. His first wife Plautia Urgulanilla gave birth to Claudius Drusus (who choked on a pear as child) and Claudia. A daughter, Antonia, was the product of his second marriage to Aelia Paetina. With Valeria Messalina (third wife) he fathered Britannicus and Octavia but had no children with Agrippina (his niece and fourth wife) who already had a son (Nero) from a previous marriage.

Healers and Healthcare

Many more physicians are known from Claudius' reign than his three predecessors: Vettius Valens; C. Stertinius Xenophon; Scribonius Largus; and Alcon. Xenophon, from the island of Cos, was Claudius' personal physician and led a very successful career with significant benefits for his family and his homeland. Epigraphic evidence indicates that he served in Britain as a military tribune being awarded a golden crown and a lance for his endeavours. He also became 'priest for life of the emperors and of Asclepius, Hygieia and Epione', according to an inscription from Cos. Subsequently, he lived on the exclusive Caelian Hill within Rome and the discovery of a pipe bearing his name suggests that he received a water supply directly from the Aqua Claudia.

Little is known of the life of Scribonius Largus, but it seems likely that he penned his major pharmaceutical work, *Compositiones medicamentorum* (The Composition of Remedies), during the period 43-48. At the time he was probably in Britain as part of Claudius' retinue and wrote: 'You will, however, forgive me if at present I describe only a few compounds to you and have not written of all diseases, for as you know we are abroad and therefore only have a moderate number of books.' But, despite this inconvenience, his collection ran to 271 chapters covering treatments within every part of the body from head to toe. He also wrote specific sections on anti-toxins, plasters and poultices, and his 300 remedies were based on 242 plants, 36 minerals and 27 animal products. Scribonius Largus provided the first clear account of opium, and it is mentioned thirty-three times within *Compositiones medicamentorum.* In addition to commenting on its use as an analgesic he described how it was made 'from the milk of the heads of wild poppies' and outlined the symptoms and the treatment of acute opium intoxication. He also quoted from Hippocrates in reminding his readers that:

> medicine is that science of healing, not harming... All gods and men should hate the doctor whose heart lacks compassion and the spirit of human kindness… Medicine does not measure a man's worth according to his wealth of character, but freely offers its help to all who seek it, and never threatens to harm anyone.

Unfortunately, some physicians fell rather short of the mark in comparison with Scribonius Largus. For example, in addition to establishing a new medical sect, Valens found time for an affair with Claudius' wife Messalina. Alcon, a specialist in treating wounds (*vulnerum medicus*) was fined a million sesterces by Claudius, presumably for over-charging patients, and banished to Gaul. Even Xenophon was implicated in the murder of Claudius.

Claudius himself seems to have been interested in the health-giving properties of plants. Pliny commented that the Bratus tree was:

> highly spoken of by Claudius, in his *History*, for its marvellous properties. He states that the Parthians sprinkle the leaves of it in their drink, that its smell closely resembles that of the cedar, and that the smoke of it is efficacious in counteracting the effects of smoke emitted by other wood.

Suetonius also quoted one of Claudius' proclamations; nothing is so effective a cure for snake bite as the juice of a yew tree'.[26]

Health Record, Diagnostic Conjectures and Historical Understanding

Suetonius made a couple of comments about Claudius' general health: 'though previously his health was bad, it was excellent while he was emperor' and 'he gave as one of his reasons for supporting a candidate for quaestorship, that the man's father had once given him cold water when he was ill and needed it'.

Two more specific health problems can be identified within the available literature – a movement disorder and upper abdominal pain.

Movement disorder

The broad term 'movement disorder' encompasses neurological conditions that can affect voluntary activities such as walking or speaking as well as causing uncontrolled (involuntary) actions. The ancient authors characterised Claudius as an individual who had difficulties with walking, speech, involuntary movements and balance. However, his intelligence was probably well above average.

Seneca in the satirical *Apocolocyntosis*, probably written a couple of months after Claudius' death, described how the recently deceased

Claudius arrived on Mount Olympus for his apotheosis (elevation to divine status) and was met by a somewhat bewildered Hercules: 'when he encountered the shape of unprecedented kind, the unusual gait, the voice like that of no land-animal but typical of sea-beasts, hoarse and inarticulate, he thought that his thirteenth labour had arrived'.

Walking

Seneca described Claudius moving 'with unequal steps' and exhibiting an 'unusual gait'. Suetonius also commented on him 'running…with his ridiculous tottering gait'.

He might also have had poor leg strength as 'when he walked, his weak knees gave way under him' and Seneca mentioned about Claudius 'dragging his right foot'. Perhaps Cassius Dio's comment on the Emperor's reliance on the use of a covered chair is further evidence of his inability to walk any significant distance. Although great care needs to be taken in deriving anatomical or medical information from coins it is of interest that nine types silver *cistophorus* from the mint of Ephesus appear to show Claudius with a wasted right leg, consistent with a weak leg.

Involuntary movements

Seneca remarked about Claudius 'wagging his head' and that he had a 'shaking hand'. Suetonius commented that 'his head was very shaky at times, but especially when he made the least exertion'. Exertion, anxiety and fatigue can certainly all increase involuntary movements.

Cassius Dio stated that 'by reason of his ill health he had frequently remained seated' and Suetonius added 'he possessed majesty and dignity of appearance, but only when he was standing still or sitting'. Claudius' preference for sitting might relate to his leg weakness or a desire to reduce the frequency of his involuntary movements.

Speech

Suetonius wrote, 'his laughter was unseemly…for he would foam at the mouth and trickle at the nose; he stammered too'. Some specific details on Claudius' speech were provided by Seneca who commented that he replied to a question 'with a confused sound and in an unintelligible voice…like that of no land animal but typical of sea beasts, hoarse and inarticulate'. Focusing on his final moments Seneca added 'This was the last utterance of his to be heard in the world, after he had let out a louder sound from that part by which he found it easier to communicate: "Oh dear, I think I've shit myself".'

Although he clearly enjoyed writing, reading his works aloud was a challenge for Claudius. Suetonius explained that 'He began to write a history in his youth…but when he gave his first reading to a large audience, he had difficulty in finishing…even while he was emperor he wrote a good deal and gave constant recitals through a professional reader'. According to Cassius Dio, 'his voice was also faltering, and he did not himself read all the measures that he introduced before the senate, but would give them to the quaestor to read, though at first, at least, he was generally present. Whatever he did read himself, he usually delivered sitting down'. As in the case of the involuntary movements, it might have been that sitting helped him to normalise his speech. According to Suetonius, the Emperor Augustus was certainly bewildered by the variability of Claudius' speech impediment: 'How… anyone who is so unclear in his conversation can speak with clearness and propriety when he declaims'.

Balance

A preference for sitting and the use of a covered chair could also suggest a balance problem. In celebrating his triumph following the invasion of Britain, it was reported that, following precedent, he ascended the steps of the Capitol on his knees but Cassius Dio reported that this was only achieved 'with his sons-in-law supporting him on either side'.

Intellect

According to Cassius Dio, 'In mental ability he was by no means inferior, as his faculties had been in constant training (in fact, he had actually written some historical treatises); but he was sickly in body, so that his head and hands shook slightly.' Suetonius mentioned his historical writing. his ability to converse in Greek and Latin in addition to 'giving no slight attention to liberal studies from his earliest youth'. It might also be that, prior to becoming Emperor, Claudius had cleverly acted the fool 'From a child he had been reared a constant prey to illness and great terror, and for that reason had feigned a stupidity greater than was really the case (a fact that he himself admitted in the senate)'.

Based on the above analysis it seems likely that Claudius had some type of movement disorder that spared his intellect and was compatible with survival into adulthood. Whether his symptoms began at birth or while an infant is unclear from the available information. However, I would argue that seeking greater diagnostic precision in modern terms beyond the broad categorisation of a 'movement disorder' is tricky. Previous attempts simply illustrate how changing modern medical contexts and ideas can influence the interpretation of historical symptoms. During the 1930s, it was commonly accepted that Claudius had suffered from poliomyelitis, by the late 1940s cerebral palsy had achieved greater favour. More recently it has been suggested that he had suffered from dystonia, Tourette's syndrome, post-polio syndrome or lead poisoning.

As a result of his disability, Claudius was distained by his relatives and Augustus' comment reported by Suetonius 'we must not furnish the means of ridiculing both him and us to a public which is wont to scoff at and deride such things' probably indicates greater concern for the public image of the Imperial family than for Claudius himself. Suetonius also added that, Augustus 'abhorred dwarfs, deformed persons and everything of that sort, as freaks of nature and of ill omen'. At the time, beauty was generally a mark of divine favour, while deformity represented the anger of the gods, being met with a blend of amusement, fascination and embarrassment. During his wilderness years, Claudius became a figure of fun within Roman high society, subject to insults and cruel tricks. Suetonius explained that Caligula 'spared him merely as a laughing stock' and once threw Claudius into a river.

It is likely that the stresses, indignities and hardships that Claudius experienced in his youth and as a young man had an impact on his character, health and behaviour. He certainly seems to have sought out and befriended other disabled individuals such as Julius Pealignus, the procurator of Cappadocia. Dice playing might have helped Claudius to cope with his solitude in addition to improving his fine motor skills. He visited the sick and as emperor demonstrated empathy by taking remedial action when he discovered, according to Suetonius, that 'certain men were exposing their sick and worn out slaves on the Island of Aesculapius because of the trouble of treating them'. But he was also portrayed as bloodthirsty and cruel, over fond of gladiatorial combat, executions and torture in addition to being easily manipulated by his wives and freedmen. Claudius was quick to anger too with Suetonius remarking that 'in hearing and deciding legal cases he showed strange inconsistency of temper, for he was now careful and shrewd, sometimes hasty and inconsiderate, occasionally silly and like a crazy man'. It has also been suggested that Claudius developed an eating disorder due to his experiences. Although gluttony is a favourite theme of Latin poets, instances of binging and vomiting – as in Claudius' case – are very rare.

Upper abdominal pain

Claudius apparently experienced attacks of stomach or oesophageal pain (*stomachi dolore*, according to Suetonius) 'which he said all but drove him to suicide'. Cassius Dio might be referring to the same problem when he wrote that, in the year before his death, 'when Claudius fell sick, Nero entered the senate and promised a horse-race in case the emperor should recover… When, now, Claudius recovered, Nero conducted the horse-race in a magnificent manner'.

Suetonius informed his readers that Claudius was something of a glutton and boozer, perhaps leading to heartburn/indigestion: 'he hardly left the dining room until he was stuffed and soaked; then he went to sleep at once, lying on his back with his mouth open, and a feather was put down his throat to relieve his stomach/oesophagus'. He might also have eaten greedily, perhaps swallowing excessive wind and Suetonius wrote that 'he is even said to have thought of an edict allowing the privilege of breaking wind quietly or noisily at table, having learned of a man who ran some risk by restraining himself through modesty'. Seneca made fun of Claudius' habit of loudly passing wind. In *Apocolocyntosis*, there is also a somewhat vague reference to Claudius having an episodic fever: 'the goddess Fever… lived with him for many years' and 'Claudius glowed white hot and… kept ordering Fever to be taken away for punishment'.

Possible modern diagnoses for Claudius severe upper abdominal pain include alcohol-induced gastritis, stomach ulceration, pancreatitis and acute cholecystitis (the latter can also produce a fever). But it is important to consider that the pain could have been heart-related too, possibly due to conditions such as angina.

Death

According to the *Apocolocyntosis*, the Emperor died quickly while being entertained by a group of comic actors between 12 noon and one o'clock on 13 October 54. Although Seneca didn't suggest that Claudius' death was due to poisoning, Pliny the Elder, writing around twenty to twenty-five years later made the following comment: 'Among the things which it is rash to eat I would include mushrooms, as although they make choice eating they have been brought into disrepute by a glaring instance of murder, being the means used to poison the Emperor Claudius by his wife Agrippina'. The poisoning story was subsequently repeated by Suetonius, Tacitus and Cassius Dio.

Suetonius

That Claudius was poisoned is a general belief, but when it was done and by whom is disputed. Some say that it was his taster, the eunuch Halotus, as he was banqueting on the Citadel with the priests, others that, at a family dinner Agrippina served the drug to him with her own hands in mushrooms, a dish of which he was extravagantly fond. Reports also differ as to what followed. Many say that as soon as he swallowed the poison he became speechless, and after suffering excruciating pain all night, died just before dawn. Some say that he first fell into a stupor, then vomited up the whole contents of his overloaded stomach, and was given a second dose, perhaps in a gruel, under pretence that he must be refreshed with food after his exhaustion, or administered in a syringe.

Tacitus

Under the weight of anxiety (*curarum*), Claudius' health broke down and he left for Sinuessa, to renovate his strength by the gentle climate and the medicinal springs. At once, Agrippina – long resolved on murder...sought advice on the type of poison... An artist in this domain was selected – a woman by name of Locusta... Her ingenuity supplied a potion, administered by the eunuch Halotus, whose regular duty was to bring in and taste the dishes ... authors of the period have recorded that the poison was sprinkled on an exceptionally fine mushroom; though, as a result of his natural sluggishness or intoxication, the effects of the drug were not immediately felt by Claudius. At the same time, a motion of his bowels appeared to have removed the danger. Agrippina was in consternation...and she fell back on the complicity...of the doctor Xenophon. He, it is believed, under cover of assisting the emperor's struggles to vomit, plunged a feather, dipped in a quick poison, down his throat.

Cassius Dio

Agrippina...made haste...by poisoning Claudius. But since, owing to the great quantity of wine he was forever drinking and his general habits of life, such as all emperors as a rule adopt for their protection, he could not easily be harmed, she sent for a famous dealer in poisons, a woman named Locusta...and preparing with her aid a poison whose effect was sure, she put it in one of the vegetables called mushrooms. Then she herself ate of the others, but made her husband eat of the one which contained the poison; for it was the largest and finest of them. And so the victim of the plot was carried from the banquet apparently quite overcome by strong drink, a thing that had happened many times before; but during the night the poison took effect and he passed away, without having been able to say or hear a word.

The precise cause of death for Claudius has been carefully considered by several modern authors. Some argue that it was a natural death due to, perhaps, cardiovascular or cerebrovascular disease, whereas others suggest that he died from poisoning (intentional or accidental) as detailed by Pliny, Suetonius, Tacitus and Cassius Dio.

Natural death

Suetonius commented on Claudius remarkably severe '*stomachi dolore*'. From the description given it is also quite possible that this could signify a heart condition akin to angina, thereby placing Claudius at heightened risk for other cardiovascular disorders such as a heart attack or a stroke. Also, at the beginning of Tacitus' description of his death he mentioned that he withdrew to Sinuessa for health reasons and, although '*curarum*' is commonly translated as anxiety it could also refer, more generally, to either 'physical or mental trouble'.

Claudius' loss of consciousness and speech are certainly compatible with a stroke. The anatomical location of the 'excruciating pain all night' mentioned by Suetonius is also not specified but, given its severity, could be cardio-vascular in origin (e.g. consistent with a heart attack or an aortic dissection). There is also evidence that individuals with movement disorders have an increased chance of developing strokes or suffering heart attacks in later life. Moreover, this risk would magnify Claudius' existing propensity to cardiovascular problems due to his poor lifestyle (obesity, excessive alcohol intake, physical inactivity and rich diet).

Murder by poisoning

In considering the odds of intentional poisoning leading to Claudius' death careful consideration needs to be given to the language used in the ancient sources, the historical context, the reported crime and the motives of the purported poisoner (Agrippina).

The language

According to Horstmanshoff, there is no Greek or Latin word that means simply 'poison'.[27] The Latin word '*venenum*' (used by Pliny, Suetonius and Tacitus) as well as the Greek 'φάρμακον' (used by Cassius Dio) require additional qualification that they are describing something harmful. Suetonius added several caveats and, although it seems likely that Claudius was given a drug by Agrippina, it is unclear if it was designed to harm or to help him. The use of the Latin word '*medicatum*' in the following extract is particularly intriguing: 'Agrippina served the drug (*medicatum*) to him with her own hands in mushrooms, a dish of which he was extravagantly fond'. Mixing foul-tasting medicines with food to make them more palatable has never been particularly unusual. Similarly, the following extract from Tacitus might be interpreted in a variety of ways given the use of the

Latin words '*venenum*' and '*medicaminis*': 'authors of the period have recorded that the poison (*venenum*) was sprinkled on an exceptionally fine mushroom; though, as a result of his natural sluggishness or intoxication, the effects of the drug (*medicaminis*) were not immediately felt by Claudius'. Both '*medicaminis*' and '*medicatum*' can also be translated as remedies or cures.

The context

It is important to consider references to poisoning within the historical context. Although very few cases of poisoning were recorded in the time of the 'five good emperors' (96–180), during the politically turbulent Julio-Claudian period there were frequent reports of poisonings. Moreover, these often implicated senior members of the imperial family and such accusations could rarely be proved or disproved.

Poisoners and their purported victims

Emperor	Suggested poisoners	Suggested imperial family victims
Augustus	Livia (wife of Augustus)	Marcellus, Gaius Caesar, Lucius Caesar, Augustus
Tiberius	Piso (assisted by poisoner, Martina) and Tiberius (accomplice). Sejanus and Livilla (wife of Drusus the Younger)	Germanicus Drusus
Caligula	Caligula Caesonia (wife of Caligula)	Tiberius Caligula
Claudius	Agrippina (assisted by poisoner Locusta)	Claudius
Nero	Nero and Agrippina (assisted by the poisoner Locusta)	Britannicus

Postmortem changes considered typical of poisoning such as darkening of the skin and early bloating but delayed putrefaction were unreliable and many so-called poisoners might have been entirely innocent. Also, the distinction between some substances acting as a poison rather than a remedy depended on the dosage and, given the poor quality of many drugs available at the time, fortuitous poisoning would not have been uncommon.

Poisoning might also have been used as a literary device to highlight a degeneration of traditional Roman values as many of the Imperial Julio-Claudian poisonings were purported to involve women. Both Locusta and Martina gained notoriety for their expertise in poisoning being linked to the deaths of Germanicus, Claudius and Britannicus. Locusta was active during the reigns of Claudius and Nero, being eventually condemned to death by the Emperor Galba. Four Imperial wives – Livia, Livilla, Caesonia and Agrippina – were implicated in poisoning their spouses. The association of poisoning with women in the ancient world might reflect perceptions as to how they could fight against powerful men. Also, the female universe was associated with magic and a knowledge of poisoning was viewed as akin to sorcery. Juvenal in his sixth satire (probably written in the late first century AD) furnished us with some evidence on Roman conceptions of gender and sexuality. Within this piece, Juvenal attacked women for their lust, pretentiousness, quarrelsomeness, lack of restraint, unsociability and superstitions. He also added that 'women love to drug and poison their husbands to get their way. The wife of Caligula drove him insane with a potion, and Agrippina poisoned Claudius.'

The crime

According to Pliny, Claudius was served poisonous mushrooms with the favoured candidate being *Amanita phalloides* (death cap) which still accounts for around 95 per cent of mushroom-related deaths. Nausea and vomiting usually occur between six and twelve hours after ingestion which can be followed by an apparent recovery. But three to six days later, the patient enters a terminal phase leading to death due to liver and kidney failure.

There has been considerable debate about exactly how the poisonous mushrooms might have been administered, given the time course. If *Amanita phalloides* is implicated then it seems more likely that Claudius received the poison earlier in the day, perhaps in a snack (of which he was extremely fond) or while he was with the priests in the Citadel. One other suggested candidate for the poisonous mushroom is *Amanita muscaria* (Fly agaric) that exerts it effects within thirty to sixty minutes of ingestion. Although this is much less poisonous than *Amanita phalloides* in most people, Claudius' pre-existing movement disorder might have made him particularly susceptible. As Juvenal pointed out, 'less guilty therefore will Agrippina's mushroom be deemed, seeing that it only stopped the breath of one old man, and sent down his palsied head and slobbering lips to heaven.'

However, Suetonius, Tacitus and Cassius Dio all suggested that a poison might have been added to the mushrooms so that they were poison*ed* rather than poison*ous*. Therefore, if Claudius was poisoned (or poisoned twice), other poisons might need to be considered such as aconite or colocynth.

According to Tacitus, Agrippina supposedly engaged the expert services of Locusta as:

> with a rapid and drastic drug, the crime, she feared would be obvious: if she decided for a slow and wasting preparation, Claudius, face to face with his end and aware of his treachery, might experience a return of affection for his son [Britannicus]. What commended itself was something recondite, which would derange his faculties while postponing his dissolution.

Guided by Agrippina's instructions, Locusta then used her female ingenuity (*muleris ingenio*) to supply a poisonous liquid (*virus*) that was poured onto (*infusum*) an exceptionally fine mushroom which Claudius presumably then ate. However, as Claudius didn't immediately succumb to Locusta's carefully formulated slow-acting poison, Agrippina apparently panicked and sought the assistance of the Imperial physician Xenophon. As detailed by Tacitus and using a feather, Xenophon then administered a second quicker acting poison to dispatch the Emperor.

Xenophon's involvement in the poisoning is somewhat bewildering given his close relationship with Claudius together with the titles and rewards that had been bestowed on him. Perhaps he is being misrepresented given the well-recorded Roman prejudice against Greek doctors. He might even have suspected poisoning and was attempting to save Claudius by getting him to regurgitate the toxic contents of his stomach. Moreover, if the poison was from *Amanita phalloides* then it would seem odd that an expert poisoner such as Locusta was unaware of the way the toxin acted. Even Seneca clearly had some inkling when he wrote 'Do you imagine that those mushrooms, the epicure's poison, work no evil results in secret, even though they have no immediate effect?'

Overall, the account provided by Tacitus hardly represents a 'professional hit' by an experienced poisoner. Moreover, Locusta subsequently poisoned Britannicus and the dramatic difference in her approach must cast doubt on the veracity of the whole Claudian episode. The problem that faced Locusta in both situations would have been to develop a formulation that acted as required and, at some point, disabled or killed the recipient. This may have entailed some testing on expendable individuals, the intended victim (at a sub-lethal dose) or on animals. Both King Mithridates VI (120-63BC) and Queen Cleopatra (69-30BC) had tried out various poisons on condemned criminals.

In the case of Britannicus, the objective was to mimic an illness from which he already suffered (*comitialis morbis*). Also, although Nero seemed to become extremely impatient with, as he saw it, Locusta's leisurely approach to the crime, it is possible to tease out three key elements which demonstrate her diligence. In the first instance, she asked one of Britannicus' tutors to test the drug on the boy, perhaps at a lower dose enabling Locusta to assess its speed of action in relation to its effects on his bowels. Suetonius wrote that Nero, presumably in conjunction with Locusta, then 'tried it on a kid, and as the animal lingered for five hours, had the mixture steeped again and again and threw some of it before a pig. The beast instantly fell dead, whereupon he ordered that the poison be taken to the dining-room and given to Britannicus.' The final stage of the poisoning was described by Tacitus as follows:

> Britannicus dined; and his food...was tried by a taster...the following expedient was discovered to avoid either changing the rule or betraying the plot by killing both master and man. A drink, still harmless, very hot and already tasted, was handed to Britannicus; then, when he declined it as too warm, cold water was poured in and with it the poison; which ran so effectively through his whole system that he lost simultaneously both voice and breath... Nero...observed that this was a usual incident due to the falling sickness (*comitialem morbum*) with which Britannicus had been afflicted from his earliest infancy...after a short silence the amenities of the banquet were resumed.

Obviously, in every poisoning there will be some elements of good (or bad) luck! Britannicus was required to judge that the drink was too warm, to request cold water to cool it and for the cold water (containing the poison) to be untested. Intriguingly, the future Emperor Titus (who dined with Brittanicus) was reported by Suetonius to have tasted the same drink and 'for a long time suffered from an obstinate disorder'. Perhaps this also illustrates how carefully Locusta had tailored the dose of the poison to her intended victim. Titus was considerably bigger than Britannicus and would have received only a tiny amount of the poison.

Overall, the process of poisoning Britannicus seems considerably more believable than that of Claudius.

The motive

It has been argued that Agrippina's motives for murdering Claudius related to concerns about the status of her marriage and the future of her son, Nero. Britannicus had also nearly reached an age where he might be viewed as the favoured candidate to succeed his biological father, Claudius. But Agrippina's senior position remained stable throughout the Emperor's tenure and both Agrippina and Nero were honoured and promoted throughout Claudius' reign. Nero's subsequent comment reported by Suetonius that mushrooms were 'the food of the gods' has been taken as suggesting some inside knowledge of Claudius' death. But perhaps it is merely a comment on the potential dangers of mushroom consumption and the deified Claudius' former penchant for them. The other major problem in suggesting that Agrippina had organised the murder was that she appeared quite unprepared for her husband's death. Suetonius mentioned that 'his death was kept quiet until all the arrangements were made about the succession. Accordingly vows were offered for his safety, as if were still ill, and the farce was kept up by bringing in comic actors, under pretence that he had asked to be entertained in that way'.

Thus, although it has been widely suggested that Claudius was poisoned by mushrooms, it seems more likely that he succumbed to a stroke or a heart attack.

CHAPTER 9

Nero

(37–68; Emperor from 54)

Nero was the son of Agrippina and Gnaeus Domitius Ahenobarbus, a man described by Suetonius as 'hateful in every walk of life'. As an infant he had to contend with both the disgrace and exile of his mother (39) followed by the death of his father (41). Subsequently, he was cared for by his Aunt Domitia and two tutors who were, claimed Suetonius, 'a dancer and a barber'.

Agrippina's return to Rome was accompanied by a dramatic improvement in both the status and the fortunes of mother and son. But, as a rising star, Nero was viewed as a threat and, according to Suetonius, 'became so prominent that...Messalina, wife of Claudius...sent emissaries to strangle him'. Messalina's concerns for the wellbeing of Britannicus were not unfounded; he was very likely poisoned by Nero.

After divorcing Messalina, Claudius wed his niece Agrippina in 49 and adopted Nero as his heir apparent two years later. Nero subsequently married Claudius' daughter, Octavia, in 53. All this enabled the 16-year-old Nero to be accepted with little opposition as Claudius' successor the following year. Nero had one child, Claudia Augusta, by his second wife Poppaea Sabina, but she died aged 4 months.

Suetonius stated that Nero's reign started well.

> Beginning with a display of filial piety, he gave Claudius a magnificent funeral, spoke his eulogy and deified him...to make his good intentions still more evident, he declared that he would rule according to the principles of Augustus, and let

> slip no opportunity for acts of generosity and mercy, or even displaying his affability.

He rejected extravagant honours, developed a constructive attitude to the senate and his administration appeared to handle judicial and financial matters wisely. However, it has been suggested that Nero was never fully in control of affairs, allowing others such as his overbearing mother Agrippina, his first wife Octavia, Burrus, prefect of the Praetorian Guard, and his tutor Seneca to act in his name. But as they all met untimely deaths between 59 and 65, Nero's actions became more unrestrained. Agrippina and Octavia were both murdered, Seneca took his own life at the request of Nero and Burrus was, as reported by Suetonius, 'sent poison...in place of a throat medicine' by the Emperor.

Nero has been characterised, like Caligula, as a narcissistic megalomaniac with a penchant for violence, murder, depravity, arson, incest and extravagance. Little better to many of his contemporaries were his passions for music, singing and drama. To the ancient authors he was viewed as someone who had deviated from the accepted norms of Roman society. In modern times he has been labelled as 'mad' suffering from psychosis, post-traumatic stress disorder or the psychiatric consequences of Cushing's Disease.

Healers and Healthcare

One of Nero's physicians, Andromachus the Elder, was best known for a mixture termed *theriac*. King Mithridates VI had previously developed a medicine to protect himself against poisoning (*mithridatium*), consisting of around forty different ingredients including opium, ginger, saffron, myrrh and cinnamon. Andromachus modified this recipe by adding in viper flesh, much more opium and increasing the number of compounds to around seventy. *Theriac* was prescribed for scores of medical problems and, over the centuries, became a remedy for virtually anything as well as protection against the, so called, '*venoms*' from poisons, snake bites and plagues.

Some doctors assisted Nero in his killings as detailed by Suetonius: 'To those who were bidden to die [Nero] never granted more than a few hours' respite, and to avoid any delay, he brought physicians who were at once to 'attend to' such as lingered; for that was the term he used for killing them by opening their veins'. Doctors played a role in the murder of Nero's aunt Domitia too by, at the Emperor's direction, 'purging the sick woman too aggressively'.

As a young man, Nero helped to promote the therapeutic properties of the thapsia plant. Pliny explained that he used to prowl the streets at night mugging or thieving and 'in his nocturnal skirmishes, it so happened that he received several contusions on his face … he anointed it with a mixture composed of thapsia, frankincense and wax, and so contrived the next day … to give lie to all rumours, by appearing with a whole skin'.

Health Record, Diagnostic Conjectures and Historical Understanding

Nero seems to have suffered from three distinct episodes of illness as emperor. Some concerns have been expressed about his appearance, vision and mental health.

Specific illness episodes

Suetonius mentioned that Nero was ill three times during his reign but that none of these was severe enough to necessitate avoiding alcohol or altering his lifestyle in any other way.

1. 60

Tacitus remarked that Nero 'had entered and swum in the sources of the stream which Quintus Marcius conveyed to Rome; and it was considered that by bathing there he had profaned the sacred waters … The divine anger was confirmed by a grave illness which followed'.

Adopting a modern perspective on Tacitus' comment it is quite possible that Nero had contracted some sort of water-borne infectious disease. However, it might also have been that Nero was visiting the 'cool and wholesome waters of the Aqua Marcia' (as described by Pliny) seeking treatment for a pre-existing illness that, unfortunately, then worsened. Augustus' physician Antoninus Musa advocated cold water remedies, a fashion that had been further popularised during the reign of Nero. Suetonius also mentioned a cold drink invented by Nero, '*Neronis decota*' that was made by boiling water and then plunging it into snow to cool. This sickness episode was both prolonged and serious as, although the visit to the Aqua Marcia can be dated to 60, Tacitus highlighted concerns about Nero's health the following year with courtiers worrying what would happen if the Emperor died.

2. 64

It has been suggested that Nero suffered from an epileptic seizure during a visit to the Temple of Vesta in 64. This is based on Tacitus' description of an episode of trembling together with Suetonius' remark about a transient visual disturbance when he stood up. There is no other available information to support such a retrospective diagnosis and both this event and a further 'funny turn' in 68 are much more in-keeping with anxiety-induced fainting.

3. 65

Philostratus wrote:

> A disease (νόσημα) broke out in Rome, called by the physicians catarrh (κατάρροος); and it was attended, it seems, by coughings, and the voice of speakers was affected by it. Now the temples were full of people supplicating the gods, because Nero had a swollen throat, and his voice was hoarse.

Νόσημα can also be translated as 'plague' and it is likely that this illness is synonymous with the disease outbreak mentioned by both Tacitus and Suetonius that apparently caused 30,000 deaths in the autumn of 65. The clinical features described by Philostratus suggest an infectious respiratory tract infection along the lines of influenza.

Appearance

The portraits of Nero on his coins changed significantly throughout his reign. One aspect that has assumed some medical significance was his progressively thickening neck accompanied by enlarging cheeks and chin. Also, according to Suetonius, 'he was of average height, his body marked with spots and malodorous, his hair light blond, his features regular rather than attractive, his eyes blue and somewhat weak, his neck over thick, his belly prominent and his legs very slender'.

It is important to appreciate that numismatic images would have been designed for a range of political and social purposes, so there is a need to tread very carefully in assigning pathology to coin portraits. However, specific suggestions have been made that Nero was either significantly overweight or was suffering from a hormonal imbalance affecting the adrenal glands, Cushing's Syndrome, which can also be associated with depression, anxiety, dramatic moods swings and psychoses.

Consistent with Suetonius' description, individuals with Cushing's Syndrome can develop facial enlargement (moon face), centripetal obesity, acne and wasting of thigh muscles. But it is a serious condition with a high death rate and patients are often troubled by diabetes, high blood pressure, thin bones (with fractures) and poor wound healing. Considering Nero's historical and health record as a whole, it seems extraordinarily unlikely that he suffered from anything akin to Cushing's Syndrome.

An alternative suggestion is that the coin images portray an individual becoming progressively obese due to overindulgence in food and drink. Nero certainly entertained well, and Tacitus commented that he even served 'banquets in public places and treated the entire city as his palace'. On the other hand, Nero was careful in looking after his health and his voice. According to Suetonius, 'he used to lie upon his back and hold a leaden plate on his chest, purge himself by clyster and by vomiting, and deny himself fruits and foods injurious to the voice.' Pliny also mentioned the lead plate and commented that 'he used to eat leeks and oil every month, upon stated days, abstaining from every other kind of food, and not so much touching so much a morsel of bread even.' The drink *Neronis decota* was a remarkably healthy concoction as it was, essentially, sterilised water!

Suetonius remarked that, Nero's general 'health was good…he was utterly shameless in the care of his person' and as well as acting and singing, he relished opportunities to participate in chariot racing or gladiatorial contests. According to Cassius Dio, following an extravagant banquet in 66, he 'publicly sang to the lyre, and also drove a chariot, clad in the costume of the Greens and wearing a charioteer's helmet'. Chariot driving was not a sport for the faint hearted, with significant strength, weight and endurance being required to control the speeding horses especially around tight bends. Both charioteers and gladiators underwent strict physical training to hone their skills, and it seems likely that Nero would have taken matters equally seriously. A strong neck is linked to upper body strength and stability improving mobility, posture as well as reducing the likelihood of injuries such as concussion. Perhaps Nero's later coin images simply depict an individual who was hefty and strong enough to drive chariots, a portrait that would undoubtedly have found favour with Nero himself.

Vision

In writing about Nero's vision both Suetonius and Pliny used the Latin verb *hebeo* suggesting some deficiency of Nero's sight. Suetonius stated that 'his eyes were blue and somewhat weak' and Pliny commented that 'Nero could see nothing distinctly without screwing up his eyes, and having it brought close to his eyes'.

It has been suggested that, like Tiberius, he was short-sighted, a condition than can be rectified by means of lenses or viewing things through a tiny aperture. Suetonius made an intriguing comment that he would view the games 'through small openings' and Pliny mentioned that he used a '*smaragdus*' when watching the fights between gladiators. The word '*smaragdus*' can be translated as a transparent precious stone of a bright green colour such an as an emerald or a green beryl, but exactly how such an object was used by Nero is unclear. It might have served as a lens, a mirror or, according to Pliny, 'refreshing [strained] eyes…soothing their feeling of fatigue'.

Mental Health

Within Act III of the tragedy *Octavia*, written shortly after the death of Nero, Agrippina laments, 'Where has your madness [*furor*] led you?' perhaps indicating something about the contemporary views concerning Nero's mental health. Tacitus, Suetonius and Cassius Dio also suggested that he was troubled by severe anxiety, for example, 'when he entered the temple of Vesta, he began to quake in every limb… possibly because the memory of his crimes never left him devoid of fear', 'he was frightened by manifest portents from dreams, auspices and omens, both old and new' and 'having learned that Galba…had revolted, he fainted and lay for a long time insensible, without a word and all but dead'.

Also, on occasions, circumstances seemed to completely overwhelm him:

> He learned of the uprising of the Gallic provinces, on the anniversary of his mother's murder, and received the news with calmness and indifference…for eight whole days making no attempt to write a reply to anyone, none to give any commission or command, he blotted out the affair with silence.
>
> Nero was informed of the uprising of Vindex as he was viewing the gymnastic contest in Neapolis…but, far from showing any grief, he leaped down from his seat and vied in prowess with some athlete. Nor did he hurry back to Rome, but merely sent

> a letter to the senate, in which he asked them to excuse him for not coming, pleading a sore throat, implying that he would like, even at this crisis, to sing to them.

Any mental health diagnosis is highly context-dependent, so it is important to be extremely cautious in suggesting specific modern diagnoses to explain Nero's behaviours such as 'post-traumatic stress disorder' or a form of psychosis. Also, as in the case of Caligula, a 'madness' narrative might have better suited Tacitus' or Suetonius' perspectives on Nero's reign. How he really responded to the infamous fire of Rome is difficult to gauge based on Tacitus' somewhat contradictory comments that 'during the burning of the palace, he was rushing unguarded from place to place in the night' and he mounted 'his private stage' and sang 'the destruction of Troy'. The *Tabula Larinas* contains part of a senatorial decree seeking to prevent individuals of senatorial class from becoming professional actors or performers. This provides a helpful window into the possible attitudes to Nero's theatricality amongst the elite of first-century Rome. His performances might even have led some to consider that, taken together with his other activities and behaviours, he was somewhat mentally unbalanced.

Throughout his life Nero cultivated interests in art, architecture, music and drama. According to Tacitus, 'Nero, even in his childish years, turned his vivacious mind to other interests: he carved, painted, practised singing or driving.' In 60 he introduced competitions in poetry, music, athletics and racing (the *Neroneia*), he performed himself in public in Naples (64) and Rome (65) followed by participation in the great festivals of Greece (66-67). Suetonius commented that even at the end of his reign and faced with revolts 'in preparing for the campaign his first care was to select wagons to carry his theatrical instruments' and in his last moments he was reported as saying, 'What an artist the world is losing.'

It might be that Nero's increasing interests in drama and music represented his way of coping with personal demons. Tacitus wrote that, in 64, 'a desire that grew every day sharper impelled Nero to appear regularly on the public stage' and, according to Cassius Dio:

> [He] threw off the dignity of his sovereignty to beg in the guise of a runaway slave, to be led about as a blind man, to be heavy with child, to be in labour, to be a madman, or to wander an outcast, his favourite roles being those of Oedipus, Thyestes, Heracles, Alcmeon and Orestes.

At the start of his reign Suetonius explained that Nero had 'left to his mother [Agrippina] the management of all public and private business' but, over the years, the relationship soured and eventually matricide was being contemplated. Nero's murder of Agrippina in 59 was a prolonged affair and after failed attempts to crush or to drown her, she was eventually stabbed to death. According to Tacitus, as 'the centurion was drawing his sword…she proffered her womb to the blow. "Strike here," she exclaimed.' Tacitus continued 'but only with the completion of the crime was its magnitude realised by [Nero]. For the rest of the night, sometimes dumb and motionless, but not rarely starting in terror to his feet with a sort of delirium, he waited for the daylight'.

Suetonius and Cassius Dio added more details to the event:

> He hurried off to view her corpse, handled her limbs…he could not either then or ever afterwards endure the stings of conscience…he was hounded by his mother's ghost and the whips and blazing torches of the Furies…his own conscience was so disturbed at night that he would leap suddenly from his bed, and by day, when he merely heard the blare of trumpets sounding forth some stirring martial strain from the region where lay Agrippina's bones, he would be terror-stricken. He therefore kept changing his residence; and when he had the same experience in the new place also, he would move in utter fright elsewhere.

Nero was clearly profoundly affected by the killing of his mother and, perhaps, his subsequent desire to engage in certain dramatic performances was linked to this. In Euripides' tragedy *Orestes*, Orestes murdered his mother Clytemnestra not just for killing Agamemnon (Orestes' father) but also because she had stolen his royal inheritance. Following the matricide, Orestes was pursued by the Furies and condemned to death until his eventual trial and acquittal in Athens. For Nero, acting out the story of Orestes might, perhaps, have been about justifying his killing of Agrippina and seeking closure.

The death of Nero's second wife, Poppaea Sabina in 65 whom he 'dearly loved', as well as their daughter Claudia Augusta two years previously, had significant impacts on him. According to Tacitus, Nero 'showed himself as incontinent in sorrow as in joy'. The exact cause of Poppaea's death is uncertain but it seems most likely than she died from a pregnancy-related condition. Tacitus wrote:

> Nero was desirous of children, and love for his wife was a ruling passion. [Poppaea's] body was…embalmed by stuffing with spices, then laid to rest in the mausoleum of the Julian race…a public funeral was held; and the emperor…eulogized her beauty, the fact that she had been the mother of an infant daughter now divine, and other favours of fortune which did duty for virtues.

Pliny also commented on the enormous quantities of perfumes burnt at the funeral. According to Cassius Dio:

> Nero missed her so greatly after her death that on learning of a woman who resembled her he at first sent for her and kept her; but later he caused a boy of the freedmen, whom he used to call Sporus, to be castrated, since he, too, resembled Poppaea, and he used him in every way like a wife. In due time…he formally 'married' Sporus.

Echoing his reaction to the death of Agrippina it might be suggested that singing 'Canace in labour' was about Nero coming to terms with the deaths of his wife and daughter. Moreover, 'the masks that he wore were sometimes made to resemble the characters he was portraying and…the women's masks were all fashioned after the features of Poppaea, in order that, though dead, she might still take part in the spectacle.'

Death

Nero's journey to suicide was a somewhat prolonged affair proceeded by troubling dreams and omens. According to Suetonius, he first obtained some poison – which was stolen – and then called for the gladiator Spiculus to kill him, but no one appeared. Then changing 'his purpose again, he sought for some retired place where he could hide and collect his thoughts'. He was next encouraged to end his life by a few remaining companions while they dug and furnished his grave. Upon discovering that he had been declared a public enemy by the Senate, he took two daggers and tested their blades, before putting them aside. Eventually, with the assistance of one of his freedmen, Epaphroditus, Nero drove a dagger into his own throat.

To some ancient authors the way in which an emperor's death was described needed to accord with the manner in which they lived, leading to some concerns about potential biases and distortions. Within the early empire, committing suicide became a moral duty for a nobleman after losing face or the favour of the emperor. It was about saving their honour and dignity (linked to the Roman concept of *virtus*) by, typically, using their own weapons against themselves.

According to Hooff,[28] the number of people engaged in self-killing peaked during the Julio-Claudian period, most commonly involving individuals at the top and the bottom of society. Several methods were used including starving, hanging, jumping, burning and poisoning but cutting seems to have been most favoured (dagger, knife, scalpel or razor). Hanging, jumping, burning were seen as less respectable and, perhaps, more 'Oriental' or 'Greek'.

Tacitus describes some other suicides during the reign of Nero and, perhaps, they serve to emphasise the somewhat chaotic and hesitant attempts of Nero. For example, Seneca had been instructed to end his life and, after getting various matters in order, embraced and reassured his wife before having his veins and arteries cut open so that he would gradually bleed to death. According to Suetonius, as he bled 'he dictated a long discourse…in the meantime, as death continued to be protracted and slow, asked Statius Annaeus, who he had long held his confidence as a loyal friend and a skilful doctor, to produce the poison'.

At the other end of the social scale was a emancipated slave named Epicharis who, Tacitus reported, 'set an example…at a time when persons freeborn and male, Roman knights and senators, untouched by torture, were betraying each his nearest and dearest.'

CHAPTER 10

Marcus Aurelius

(121–180; Emperor from 161)

When Marcus Aurelius was only 3, his biological father died and he was then raised by his mother and grandfather. When Hadrian adopted Antoninus Pius as his successor, the *SHA* reported that the agreement was framed in such a way that Antoninus concomitantly 'adopted Marcus Aurelius, the son of his wife's brother, and Lucius Verus, the son of Aelius Verus'. Although Antoninus Pius had probably been viewed as a caretaker emperor by Hadrian, he confounded expectations and ruled for twenty-three years, with Marcus Aurelius serving a prolonged apprenticeship. Facilitated by a frugal lifestyle the elderly emperor remained remarkably fit into old age and Marcus Aurelius later commented that 'he looked after himself so successfully that he was seldom in need of medical attention'.

He commenced his reign as joint emperor with Lucius Verus but, after a very brief honeymoon period, he was confronted by several enormous challenges. As well as becoming embroiled in wars in the East and the North he also had to contend with the Antonine Plague, the sudden death of Lucius Verus and the revolt of Cassius. He married Antoninus' daughter Annia Galeria Faustina in 145 and they had fourteen children. However, only one son (the future Emperor Commodus) and four daughters outlived him. His wife was also frequently accused of infidelity.

Health and Healthcare

The physician Galen has already been discussed in relation to his professional background and some of his recommended treatments.

Although he has often been characterised as verbose, arrogant, impatient and judgemental, his contributions to medicine and philosophy were colossal. He may have written as many as 500 treatises amounting to around 10 million words, of which at least 3 million still survive today.

Aside from his literary output, Galen's other claim to fame concerned his association with Marcus Aurelius. In addition to serving as Imperial physician, Galen also shared the Emperor's interests in Stoic philosophy. He was certainly no stranger to loss, with his father dying when Galen was 19. The Antonine Plague then took away several friends in addition to all his slaves and, subsequently, a great fire consumed a large portion of his library (including many of his own works), medicines and possessions.

In his book *De tranquillitate animi* (Avoiding Distress), Galen reflected on these events and described how he had coped with living under the brutal Emperor Commodus:

> You yourself, I believe, are convinced that the crimes committed by Commodus in a few years are worse than any in the whole of recorded history. So when I saw all of these things happening daily, I schooled my imagination to prepare for the loss of everything that I had… I also expected to be sent to a desert island, like other innocent victims… I advise you to train your soul's imagination to cope with almost any turn of events.

Like many Romans of his time, Galen was particularly attracted to Stoicism, based on the teachings of the Hellenistic philosopher Zeno (333–261BC), writing:

> We should be amazed, if at all, at those who are not upset even when they have lost everything, like Zeno of Citium, who, they say, at the report of a shipwreck in which he had lost everything, remarked, 'You've done us a favour, Fate, by driving us to the philosopher's cloak and the Stoa'.

Zeno's ideas were taken up and modified by the Romans with a particular emphasis on the attainment of virtue. Virtue was about 'living in accordance with nature', with an emphasis on using reason and acting for the common good. The Stoics suggested that, although we share many instincts with other animals, our ability to think rationally is what makes us human. Some key individuals involved in the Romanisation of Zeno's Stoic philosophy were Seneca, Epictetus and Marcus Aurelius. They argued that a life plagued with negative emotions such as anger, anxiety (including social anxiety), grief, fear (e.g. of old age and dying) and envy would not be a good life. But the Roman Stoics did not, unlike their fellow Cynics, spurn creature comforts.

A particular challenge highlighted by Marcus Aurelius in his *Meditations* was desiring or seeking things that were not within human control such as fame, riches, immortality or reputation. There was a requirement to appreciate that life was unpredictable and most things that happened were not up to individuals, emphasising that 'Impermanence is the badge of each and every one; and yet you chase after them, or flee from them, as though they were to endure for all eternity'. Specifically in relation to other people's opinions and attitudes, Marcus Aurelius wrote, 'Begin each day by telling yourself: Today I shall be meeting with interference, ingratitude, insolence, disloyalty, ill-will, and selfishness – all of them due to the offenders' ignorance of what is good or evil.'

Health record

It has been suggested that Marcus Aurelius suffered from poor health for much of his adult life. The author of the *SHA* commented that although in his youth he was active and robust – 'He was fond of boxing and wrestling and running and fowling, played ball very skilfully, and hunted well' – it was reported that his health subsequently deteriorated; 'so much work and labour did he devote to his studies that he impaired his health'. Cassius Dio commented that 'as a result of his close application and study he was extremely frail in body, though in the beginning he had been so vigorous that he used to fight in armour … he did not meet with the good fortune that he deserved, for he was not strong in body.'

General health

Cassius Dio provided an overview of Marcus Aurelius' general health:

> He was so frail in body that at first he could not endure the cold…and he took but very little food and that always at night. It was never his practice to eat during the daytime, unless it were some of the drug called theriac. This drug he took, not so much because he feared anything, as because his stomach and chest were in bad condition; and it is reported that this practice enabled him to endure both this and other maladies.

On the face of it, Cassius Dio was well qualified to write about Marcus Aurelius being a younger contemporary with senatorial links. But the period of his *History of Rome* that deals with Marcus' reign is only available in the eleventh-century *Epitome* by Xiphilinus and in some Byzantine excerpts, so caution needs to be exercised in placing too much reliance on this text. However, in constructing a detailed health record for Marcus, three contemporaneous sources furnish complementary perspectives on his illnesses alongside the historical information provided by Cassius Dio, the *SHA* and Herodian: Marcus' correspondence with Fronto, the *Meditations* and some writings attributed to the physician Galen (*On Hygiene, On Prognosis, On Antidotes* and *On Theriac, For Piso*).

Illnesses

Correspondence between Marcus Aurelius and Fronto

Fronto (c.90-95–c.167) was Marcus Aurelius' tutor between 139 and 145, during which time they embarked on an extensive correspondence that included discussions about their respective health problems.[29]

After this period, Fronto and Marcus Aurelius kept in touch, but their communications became less frequent. Two categories of health problems affecting Marcus Aurelius can be discerned from the correspondence – primary and secondary.

Primary health problems

Three consecutive letters written by Marcus Aurelius, dated to between 143 and 147, provide some information on his health problems as a young man.

> I think I must have taken a chill [*perfrixisse*], whether from walking about in slippers in the early morning, or from writing badly, I know not. I only know that, rheumy [*pituitosus*] enough at all times, I seem to be more drivelling [*mucculentior*] than ever today. So I will pour the oil on my head and go off to sleep, for not a drop of it do I intend to pour into my lamp today, so tired am I with riding and sneezing [*sternutation*].[30]

> I slept somewhat late owing to my slight cold [*perfrictiunculam*], which seems now to have subsided … I relieved my throat, I will not say by gargling – though the word *gargarisso* is, I believe, found in Novius and elsewhere – but by swallowing honey water as far as the gullet and ejecting it again.

> My present condition you can easily gauge by the shakiness of my handwriting. As far as my strength is concerned, it is certainly beginning to come back. The pain in my chest, too, is quite gone; but that wretched sore is still irritating my throat [*ulcus autem illud* ἀπεργα…τῆς ἀρτηρίας]. I am under treatment and taking every care…my protracted illness can be made more bearable only by…strict obedience to the doctors' orders. Besides, it were shame, indeed, that a disease of the body should outlast a determination of the mind to recover health.[31]

The illnesses described by Marcus Aurelius in the three letters have some features in common with a sinus infection (i.e. runny nose, sore throat, headache, cough and fever). Pouring oil on the head was a treatment recommended by Celsus. But I would suggest that the young Marcus Aurelius may also have been magnifying the importance of his medical symptoms for the benefit of his tutor. In another letter written around the same time, he even states that 'I have used up all my breath [*spiritum insumpsi*] by dictating nearly thirty letters'.

In the first letter, the specific choice of the word '*perfrixisse*' would suggest a more serious condition than a mere 'sniffle' ('to grow very cold', 'to catch cold' are alternatives translations). Celsus wrote, 'he who has been much chilled [*perfixit*] should first sit in the caldarium, well-wrapped up, until he sweats; next be anointed.' This letter also refers to sneezing (*sternutation*) which was sometimes viewed as a more significant symptom in the ancient world – both medically and as an omen. For example, Frontinus (c.35–c.103) wrote in *Stratagems*, 'When Timotheus was about to contend…in a naval battle, his pilot, hearing one of the rowers sneeze, started to give the signal for retreat.' According to Celsus, the medical significance of sneezing depends on the context, and can be associated with nasal, throat and lung disorders. In an individual with fever, he wrote 'among good signs are: sneezing, also a desire for food'. But in pulmonary disease with sputum, he stated that 'the following are signs of danger: cough, catarrh, and even sneezing, which in other maladies is held salutary.'

The second letter is also consistent with Celsus' reported treatment for throat problems by mentioning gargling and the use of honey. But this missive is also an interaction between a tutor and his pupil, with Marcus Aurelius agonising over the use of the correct terminology, perhaps to impress his teacher, even when sick. According to Freisenbruch, the corpus of letters between Marcus Aurelius and Fronto is, to some extent, 'a correspondence course in how to be a good wordsmith, a good emperor, a good pupil'.[32]

The chest pain mentioned in the third letter was no longer present at the time of writing, so it is of doubtful significance and might have been due to persistent coughing associated with a throat problem. The medical relevance of the comment: 'shakiness of my handwriting' is more difficult to gauge. Freisenbruch takes the view that 'whether the letter-writer writes in his own hand, or employs another, does not merely reflect the health of the writer, but is also an eagerly scrutinized barometer of credibility and recognition for the recipient'.[33] However, any failure to produce an autographed communication was usually explained away by poor health and, perhaps, a temporary change in writing style can be linked to transient problems such as fever or acute anxiety.

Secondary health problems

A particularly intriguing aspect of the correspondence is how the adverse health experiences of Fronto seem to have impacted on the wellbeing of Marcus Aurelius too. Intriguingly Marcus Aurelius' reaction appears to encompass both psychological and physical elements. Two letters from him to Fronto, dating from the mid-140s and the mid-160s respectively, serve to illustrate this phenomenon.

> You may banter, but with your last letter you have sent considerable anxiety and great suffering, not to mention the most burning pain and fever, to the point that I can take no pleasure in eating, sleeping or even studying... Farewell, my teacher, whose health makes my health unimpaired and secure.

> I have just heard of your misfortune. Suffering anguish as I do when a single joint of yours aches, my master, what pain do you think I feel when it is your heart that aches? Under the shock of the news I could think of nothing else than to ask you to keep safe for me the sweetest of masters, in whom I find a greater

solace for this life than you can find for your sorrow from any source. I have not written with my own hand because after my bath in the evening even my hand was shaky.

The following dialogue between them illustrates how Marcus Aurelius' primary health problems – such as a resolving feverish illness – were influenced by Fronto's wellbeing too:

Fronto to Marcus as Caesar
I am anxious to know, my Lord, how you are keeping. I have been seized with pain in the neck.

Marcus Aurelius to Fronto
I think I have got through the night without fever. I have taken food without repugnance and am doing very nicely now. We shall see what the night brings. But, my master, by your late anxiety you can certainly gauge my feelings when I learnt that you had been seized with pain in the neck.

Marcus Aurelius to Fronto
If the pains in your neck get better, even in two days' time, it will help on my convalescence more than anything, my master. I have had a bath and today even done a little walking and taken a little more food, but not as yet without discomfort.

Marcus Aurelius to Fronto
I cannot but be distressed that at the very time when you were writing to me your neck was so painful, nor indeed do I wish to be, nor ought I to be, other than distressed. As for me, thanks be to the Gods and your prayers, I have bathed to-day, and taken sufficient food, and wine too I have used with relish.

The *Meditations*

The *Meditations* of Marcus Aurelius was not intended for public consumption, and it must be distinguished from the imperial *commentarii* produced by several previous emperors designed to showcase their strengths and achievements. It was not an idealised portrait of Marcus Aurelius but a reflective notebook for his own private use. The work was probably written between 170 and 180 when he was campaigning in Germany.

There are some allusions to specific health issues in the *Meditations:*

Pain and Chronic Ailments:
Apollonius schooled me to meet spasms of acute pain … and the tedium of a chronic ailment with the same unaltered composure.

Limb Pain:
For hand or foot to feel pain is no violation of nature, so long as the foot does its own appointed work, and the hand its own. Similarly pain for a man, as man, is no unnatural thing so long as he does a man's appointed work.

Pain:
Of Pain. If it is past bearing, it makes an end of us; if it lasts, it can be borne. The mind, holding itself aloof from the body, retains its calm, and the master-reason remains unaffected. As for the parts injured by the pain, let them, if they can, declare their own.

Pain:
When in pain, always be prompt to remind yourself that there is nothing shameful about it and nothing prejudicial to the mind at the helm, which suffers no injury either in its rational or its social aspect. In most cases the saying of Epicurus should prove helpful, that 'Pain is never unbearable or unending, so long as

> you remember its limitations and do not indulge in fanciful exaggerations'. Bear in mind also, that, though we do not realise it, many other things which we find uncomfortable are, in fact, of the same nature as pain: feelings of lethargy, for example, or a feverish temperature, or loss of appetite. When inclined to grumble at any of these, tell yourself that you are giving in to pain.
>
> Spitting Blood and Dizziness/Vertigo:
> I was given antidotes … and against the spitting [πτύειν] of blood [αἷμα] and vertigo [ἰλιγγιᾶν]. [Vertigo is quite a specific modern medical term and ἰλιγγιᾶν is probably better translated as 'to be or to become dizzy'].

It is also important to consider any health-related comments in the context of Marcus Aurelius' interests in Stoicism. Statements such as 'everything that happens is as normal and expected as the spring rose and the summer fruit; this is true of sickness, death, slander, intrigue' indicate that Marcus, as a Stoic philosopher, was working out how to cope with a range of challenges outside his control including illnesses. He also wrote that 'Maximus was my model for self-control, stability of purpose and cheerfulness under ill-health and other misfortunes.'

Given the nature of the *Meditations*, it seems unlikely that any of the comments on Marcus' health were embellished but it might be that some elements were downplayed because of his Stoic perspective. To a Stoic, health and wealth are preferred indifferents and Marcus' approach was to strip away the reputation and appeal of such indifferents in order to focus on the virtues of gentleness, courage, truthfulness, good faith, simplicity and self-sufficiency. He also emphasised the greater importance of the mind compared to the body, writing: 'it is disgraceful if, in this life, when your body does not give up the struggle, your mind should do so first'. He differentiated between the ability to control one's mind (and therefore actions) but not the actions of the body and used a diminutive form ('the poor/mere body') to emphasise the low status of the body.

It has been argued that the *Meditations* as a whole sheds some light on both the personality and the health of Marcus Aurelius. Some have interpreted the frequent self-criticisms within the text as a sign that he suffered from an identity crisis. Others have suggested that he had a pessimistic personality disorder associated with despair and doubt leading to the development of various psychosomatic disorders and hypochondriasis. Cassius Dio's comment that 'his stomach and chest were in bad condition' has, for example, been scrutinised in relation to the *Meditations* by Dailly and Van Effenterre. Based on their conjecture that Marcus Aurelius had a gastric ulcer, they suggested that he would have exhibited anxiety and unease as part of his stomach-related condition with an inclination to search for justifications; hence the production of the *Meditations*.[34]

Cassius Dio's comment 'It was never his practice to eat during the daytime, unless it were some of the drug called *theriac*', has also been linked to content of the *Meditations*. By the time of Marcus Aurelius, *theriac* consisted of around seventy individual ingredients, including opium, and it has been suggested that Marcus Aurelius was suffering from symptoms of opium intoxication. Various passages within the *Meditations* have also been cited as evidence of opium-related cognitive disturbances or hallucinations, for example: 'Time is a river, the resistless flow of all created things. One thing no sooner comes in sight than it is hurried past and another is borne along, only to be swept away in its turn.'

But it is argued that all these interpretations of the *Meditations* are both anachronistic and misrepresent the broad purpose of Marcus Aurelius' writings. Hadot wrote, 'Marcus' seemingly pessimistic declarations are not expressions of disgust or disillusion at the spectacle of life; rather they are a means he employs in order to change his way of evaluating the events and objects which go to make up human existence.'[35] Perhaps Marcus Aurelius' thinking was also in line with mainstream Stoicism in that he was undertaking a critical analysis of himself and his life with a view to self-improvement. Gill concluded that the work is consistent with 'the idea of the life of a committed Stoic as an ongoing journey towards an ideal state of character or understanding'.[36]

Van Ackeren focused on Marcus Aurelius' specific use of self-reflection and self-dialogue in the *Meditations.* He considered that these elements are a unique aspect of Marcus Aurelius' practical approach to Stoicism (in comparison with, for example, Epictetus and Seneca) as opposed to suggesting anything about his personality, psychological well-being or physical health.[37]

Galen's writings

The physician Galen's association with the imperial household commenced in 168 but he probably didn't meet Marcus Aurelius in person until 176. In the interim he was appointed to prepare theriac for the Emperor following the death of the Imperial doctor Demetrius.

One specific medical episode during 176 involving Marcus Aurelius is detailed in *On Prognosis* (*De Praecognitione*):

> Now the cure that I performed on the emperor himself was really remarkable. He and the medical advisors who had accompanied him on campaign believed a paroxysm of fever had begun, but they were all proved wrong… On the previous day he had taken a draught of bitter aloes at the first hour and then some theriac at about the sixth, as was his daily custom. He had a bath at sunset and a light meal. All night long there followed colicky pains and evacuations through the lower belly, which made him feverish, and when the court doctors saw him in the morning, they advised him to rest and fed him some thick gruel at the ninth hour…an emissary from the emperor came to summon me... It seemed to me that his pulse, compared with the general

> norm for each age and constitution, was far from showing the onset of an attack of illness, and so I said there was no attack of fever, but his stomach was overloaded with the food he had taken, which had turned to phlegm before excretion, and that was now quite clear... I should have prescribed my usual dose of wine with pepper on top...but it was enough to place over the mouth of the stomach a pad of wool impregnated with warm nard ointment.

A likely modern diagnostic equivalent of the disease being described is infective gastroenteritis which, in general, benefits from minimal medical intervention. Within the broader text, Galen also clearly delighted in detailing the praises heaped on him by the Emperor, adding 'he was continually speaking of me as the first among physicians and unique among philosophers'. Therefore, it is quite possible that Galen was somewhat economical with the truth in reporting the actions of Marcus Aurelius' other physicians with whom he treated the Emperor, perhaps embellishing his own role. However, he would also have been extremely wary of making any mistakes, so producing a diagnosis of a relatively minor disorder and offering gentle therapy is of particular significance.

Diagnostic Conjectures and Historical Understanding

Minor ailments and self-limiting conditions

The historical evidence indicates that Marcus Aurelius suffered from possible sinus infections (with colds and sore throats), occasional gastroenteritis plus various aches and pains but there is no suggestion that he was troubled by any significant or chronic health problems. Despite the fact that Cassius Dio wrote that Marcus Aurelius was weak and frail, he also commented that 'To be sure, he could not display many feats of physical prowess; yet he had developed his body from a very weak one to one capable of the greatest endurance'. Two extracts have been identified concerning chest pain and spitting blood but both of these symptoms can be associated with a range of conditions of varying seriousness. Moreover, in the case of Marcus Aurelius, these were isolated episodes that seem to have resolved with no reported associations or sequalae.

Another entry in Cassius Dio in relation to a rebellion in 175 translates as follows:

> But Cassius in rebelling made a terrible mistake, due to his having been deceived by Faustina. The latter, who was the daughter of Antoninus Pius, seeing that her husband had fallen ill and expecting that he would die at any moment, was afraid that the throne might fall to some outsider.

This could be interpreted as an acute or chronic illness or – and perhaps more likely – that Marcus Aurelius was normally fit and well; suddenly falling ill was particularly shocking for Faustina, and she over-reacted.

More broadly, Marcus Aurelius' health record highlights the challenges of diagnosing minor ailments and self-limiting conditions in important historical figures. There may be a tendency to consider that an ill or incapacitated ruler must always have a serious condition (possibly exacerbated by some defensive medical practice being undertaken by their contemporary carers as indicated by Galen's report).

Marcus Aurelius was certainly committed to following a healthy lifestyle as demonstrated by the following:

> In the *Meditations* he outlined the qualities he admired in his adoptive father, Antonius Pius, including the way he looked after himself. In the following paragraph he also thanked the gods for granting him such prolonged resistance when he lived rough, sleeping in tents on the banks of the Danube.

> In a letter to Fronto he wrote 'I have dictated this walking about. For the state of my wretched body requires exercise just now.'
>
> In his book *On Hygiene*, Galen cited Marcus Aurelius as an exemplar explaining how 'he attended most promptly to the care of his body, came to the wrestling school at sunset on the short days, and on the longest days at the ninth or, at the latest, the tenth hour'.

While the secondary health problems identified in some of the communications between Marcus Aurelius and Fronto also don't suggest any serious medical issues, they are of broader interest. Although there is evidence for empathy and compassion in the medicine and literature of the first and second centuries, Marcus Aurelius' reactions to Fronto's predicaments seem to amount to a more excessive form. Extreme empaths might not only experience what the other person feels but suffer it too. Moreover, an excess of empathy can be associated with difficulties in managing emotions and blunts an individual's ability to recognise psychotic or manipulative behaviour in others. Perhaps Marcus Aurelius' extreme empathy and Stoicism contributed to him being overly tolerant of the reported excesses of his co-emperor, Lucius Verus, the alleged infidelities of his wife and the behaviour of his son and successor Lucius Commodus.

Theriac dependence

Galen wrote about the Emperor's use of theriac: 'For his safety every day he took as much as an Egyptian *kyamos* [bean] with or without water or wine'. Marcus Aurelius' daily consumption of theriac might have been about protecting himself against poisoning – as implied by Galen's use of the term 'safety'. In his book *On the Usefulness of Parts of the Body*, Galen also broadly classified theriac as an antidote against poisons, venoms and diseases caused by a bad diet. Moreover, in the context of the Antonine Plague that was ravaging the Roman

Empire during the reign of Marcus Aurelius, Galen commented that theriac was 'the only [thing] able to help those who drink it, no other form of help being constituted in such a way as to resist an evil of such magnitude'.

Marcus Aurelius became an exemplar for others too:

> For there are healthy men who take theriac without interruption throughout their whole life…some take the drug every day for the good of their body; we know that the divine Marcus Aurelius…because of the close and intelligent attention he paid to the constitution of his body used the drug greedily and as if it were a food. For because of him the drug became more widely known and the power of its action became clearer to men. For from the state of health which the emperor acquired the antidote gained increased faith in its power.

The amount of opium that Marcus was consuming within the theriac was probably quite low; figures of 1.52mg and 3.3mg per day have been suggested.[38] But, although it seems unlikely that Marcus Aurelius was – in modern terms – an opium addict, it might be that he had some degree of dependence on theriac based on the following:

Food-like ingestion (suggesting desire to take theriac for the sense of wellbeing it engendered)
Galen indicated that he 'used the drug greedily and as if it were a food' and Cassius Dio wrote that it was 'never his practice to eat during the daytime, unless it were some of the drug called theriac'.

Insomnia (suggesting possible psychic dependence)
Galen commented, 'When he found himself getting drowsy in his duties, he had the poppy juice removed [from the theriac]. But then he was unable to sleep at night…so he was obliged to

have recourse again to the compound which contained poppy-juice.'

Scrutiny of the production of theriac

Irrespective of his enormous imperial workload, Marcus exhibited an unusually keen interest in the manufacture and supply of the theriac for his personal use. Galen also wrote that 'when he returned to Rome [Marcus] enquired about the proportions of simple medicines I used in my preparation [of theriac]', and he had to reassure the Emperor that the formulation was identical to that made up by his previous physician, Demetrios.

Death

Herodian described the terminal decline in the health of Marcus Aurelius: 'exhausted not only by age but also by labours and cares, he suffered a serious illness while visiting the Pannonians'. Subsequently, he 'suffered a severe fainting spell and sank back on his couch, exhausted by weakness and worry... After living another night and day, Marcus died.'

And, according to the *SHA*:

> He passed away in this fashion...he gradually became sick... then, being keen to expire, he abstained from eating and drinking, and so provoked the illness... On the sixth day he called his friends and said to them 'Why do you cry for me, instead of considering the pestilence, and the death that is the common destiny of all of us?' On the seventh day he was tired and gave access only to his son, and even he was sent away because of fear that he would catch [*transiret*] the disease. And when his son had departed, he concealed his head as though he desired sleep and in the night he took his last breath.

Cassius Dio adopted a slightly different perspective on Marcus Aurelius' demise:

> He passed away on the seventeenth of March, not as a result of the disease from which he still suffered, but by the act of his physicians, as I have been plainly told, who wished to do Commodus a favour. When now he was at the point of death, he commended his son to the protection of the soldiers (for he did not wish his death to appear to be due to Commodus).

It might be suggested that Marcus Aurelius died relatively prematurely at 58 in comparison with the proceeding eight emperors who had passed away naturally at an average age of 67. But taking a larger sample and including all thirty Roman and Byzantine rulers who had died from natural causes (from Augustus to Heraclius) Marcus Aurelius' survival was closer to the mean of sixty years.

Throughout his time as Emperor, Marcus Aurelius was subject to enormous burdens and adversities that are likely to have impacted on his physical and mental wellbeing. Three-quarters of his nineteen-year reign was taken up with fighting in the East or on the Northern frontiers. While his co-emperor, Lucius Verus, took responsibility for the campaign in Parthia (162-166), Marcus himself spent around ten years away from Rome campaigning against the Quadi, Marcomanni and Iazyges in Germany (168-176 and 178-180). In addition, he had to cope with natural disasters (flood and famine in Rome (161) and the Antonine Plague (166-185)), hostile invasions of Italy and Greece (170-171) and an insurrection in the East (175).

The brutality of Marcus Aurelius' final years on the Northern Frontier can, perhaps, still be gleaned today by comparing the reliefs on the Columns of Marcus Aurelius and Trajan in Rome. The emphasis on construction and care (including healthcare) that is detailed on Trajan's column (built 113) is absent from that of Marcus Aurelius (built 193). On the latter, scenes of violent battles and cruelties prevail.

It does not seem unreasonable to suggest that, by 180, Marcus Aurelius was, in the words of Herodian 'exhausted by weakness and worry'. However, in relation to his final days, consideration must also be given to the comments in the *SHA* about a 'pestilence' and sending Commodus away 'because of fear that he would catch the disease'. Thus, it is possible that Marcus was a victim of the Antonine Plague that had spread over the Empire from the East during his reign. But Cassius Dio's final comment is important to consider too: 'he passed away on the seventeenth of March, not as a result of the disease from which he still suffered, but by the act of his physicians, as I have been plainly told, who wished to do Commodus a favour'. Dismissing the political slur on Commodus, it is suggested that this extract acquires greater significance in association with another passage from the *SHA*: 'being keen to expire, he abstained from eating and drinking, and so provoked the illness'.

Perhaps, at the end, an exhausted Marcus Aurelius was seeking to terminate his own life by means of starvation/dehydration and/or with the assistance of his physicians. He certainly would have had access to opium as a component of his regular theriac dose. And, to quote Pliny, 'Opium is not only soporific, but if too large a dose be swallowed the sleep even ends in death… In this way, we are told, died the father of Publius Licinius…when an unbearable illness had made life hateful to him, and so also several others.'

CHAPTER 11

Lucius Verus

(130–169; Co-Emperor from 161)

Lucius Verus was the eldest son of Lucius Aelius Caesar who, having been chosen by Hadrian as his successor in 136, died two years later aged 36. Subsequently Lucius Verus was adopted by Antoninus Pius alongside Marcus Aurelius. He was co-emperor with Marcus Aurelius from 161 until his sudden death eight years later. Between 162 and 166 he led the Roman campaign in the east against the Parthian Empire of the Arsacids.

Not only was Lucius nine years younger than Marcus Aurelius, but he was considered to be physically fitter and more robust. Cassius Dio described him as 'a vigorous man of younger years and better suited for military enterprises'. He married Marcus Aurelius' daughter Annia Lucilla, producing three children, two of whom died young. Lucius Verus' lifestyle was also quite different from that of Marcus Aurelius. According to the *SHA*, he overindulged in food and alcohol, even having a tavern built in his house where he spent his time gambling, eating, drinking and eventually 'falling asleep on the banqueting-couch, so that he would be lifted up with the covers and carried to his bedroom'.

Healers and Healthcare: The Antonine Plague

The major health-related event linked to Lucius Verus was the Antonine Plague. According to the *SHA*, following the conclusion of the Parthian War:

> He appeared to bring the plague with him into those provinces through which he made his return journey as far as Rome. The pestilence is reported to have arisen in Babylonia, when a pestilential vapour escaped from a golden casket in the temple of Apollo, which a soldier had by chance cut open; and thence it filled the Parthians' land and the world.

The effects of this illness were dramatic and, although estimates vary, it is suggested that it led to at least 3-5 million deaths. In some areas it might have killed as many as one-third of the population and weakened the Roman army for a generation. There were economic impacts too, with evidence for concomitant declines in agricultural production, tree-felling, silver and lead mining as well as the minting of coins.

The physician Galen encountered the plague at several points in his career. He was in Rome when it arrived in 166 and, during a visit to Aquileia on behalf of Emperor Marcus Aurelius in 168-169, he wrote:

> The plague attacked more destructively than even before, so the emperors fled immediately to Rome with a small force of men. For the rest of us, survival became very difficult for a long time. Most, indeed, died, the effects of the plague being exacerbated by the fact that all of this was occurring in the middle of winter.

Aristides, a sophist from Smyrna, also provided us with a patient's perspective:

> A plague infected nearly all my neighbours. First two or three of my servants grew sick, then one after another. Then all were in bed, both the younger and the older. I was last to be attacked... The livestock too became sick...little by little with trouble and difficulty I recovered. The fever did not leave me completely until the most valued of my foster children died.

Dio Cassius, who was a young man at the time, described the disease: 'A pestilence occurred, the greatest of any of which I have knowledge; for two thousand persons often died in Rome in a single day.' Herodian, writing after the end of the plague, also provided some fascinating detail on the pandemic and contemporary thoughts on its causes and treatment:

> About this time, plague struck all Italy. The suffering was especially severe in Rome, since the city, which received people from all over the world, was overcrowded. The city suffered great loss of both men and animals…on the advice of his physicians, Commodus left Rome for Laurentum…to counteract the pollution in the air by the fragrant scent of the laurels and the refreshing shade of the trees. At the direction of their doctors, those who remained in Rome filled their nostrils and ears with fragrant oils and used perfume and incense constantly, for some said that the sweet odour, entering first, filled up the sensory passages and kept out the poison in the air; or, if any poison should enter, it would be neutralized by the stronger odours. The plague, however, continued to rage unchecked for a long time, and many men died, as well as domestic animals of all kinds. Famine gripped the city at the same time.

Galen was also directly involved in the care of patients suffering from the Antonine Plague but he did not, unfortunately, write a specific account of the diagnostic characteristics of the disease, being more focused on treatments. However, within his writings, it is possible to tease out some important clinical features from his scattered comments: skin changes, fever, bowel and stomach symptoms in addition to coughing.

Most detail is provided on the skin rashes, and three ancient Greek nouns were used by Galen in his descriptions: ἐξάνθημα (pustules/eruption); ἐφελκίς (scab or a sore/wound); ἕλκος (wound/sore/ulcer). The modern medical term exanthem is derived directly from the Greek ἐξάνθημα (exanthema) which means 'a breaking out'. ἄνθος (anthos) in Greek is 'flower' particularly a 'flower blossom', so a patient breaking out with a rash is likened to a flower bursting into bloom. However, in the context of first- and second-century Rome, it is important to consider how the word was being used by contemporary medical writers. For example, Celsus explained: 'Pustules arise chiefly in the spring; there are many kinds. For at times a sort of roughness comes all over the body, or a part of it, resembling the pustules which are set up by nettles or by sweating; ἐξάνθημα the Greeks call them'.

Galen wrote: 'At that time, a young man broke out in pustules/sores [ἐξάνθημα/ἕλκος] over his whole body on the ninth day, just as did almost all the others who were saved.' In terms of the natural history of the exanthemata, Galen also added that 'in some, in whom there was also ulceration, the surface fell off, which they call scabs [ἐφελκίς] … and after one or two days scarred over. In others, in whom there was no ulceration, the pustules [ἐξάνθημα] were rough and itchy, and fell off like something scaly.' Elsewhere Galen explained how sometimes the 'whole body breaks out all over in black pustules. Sometimes these fall off like scales, when they had dried and subsided, but only gradually'.

Galen's description of the rash (in the context of a fever) suggests that it represented a condition akin to modern-day smallpox. Other possibilities that have been proposed include measles, epidemic typhus and typhoid but the skin changes of smallpox are much more consistent with Galen's description of his patients suffering from the Antonine Plague.

Modern reported skin changes in smallpox, measles, typhus and typhoid

	Smallpox	Measles	Epidemic typhus	Typhoid
Skin changes	Red spots developing into sores. These become pea-like pustules and, then, scabs which are eventually shed	Flat red spots, sometimes including small raised bumps	Flat red spots	Flat rose-coloured spots in a third of patients
Skin rash distribution	Starts in the mouth and on the face, spreading to the rest of body	Starts in the mouth and on the face, spreading to the neck, trunk and extremities	Commences on the trunk and spreads to the rest of body	Lower chest and abdomen

But, in relation to the clinical information available from Galen, it is important to appreciate that what has survived is probably only a small portion of the original literature on the Antonine Plague. There might have been a bias in the reporting and recording of certain symptoms linked to the purposes (and likely audience) of the surviving sources alongside contemporary views about the aetiology and nature of a plague. Malnutrition amongst the population within Rome might also have confounded any link between some clinical features (as described in modern medical sources) and smallpox.

However, one of the overarching concerns about equating the variola virus (VARV) responsible for modern smallpox with the organism causing the Antonine Plague is that, over a period of 1,800 years, the genetic structure of some viruses might have been altered by random mutations thereby changing its biological behaviour. If this is the case in relation to the evolutionary history of our modern-day variola virus then it raises some doubts about the retrospective diagnostic relevance of Galen's clinical description.

VARV is a species within the orthopoxvirus genus alongside the vaccinia virus, the cowpox virus and the monkeypox virus. Comparisons of the VARV genome to those of the most closely related orthopoxviruses suggests that it is a relatively young species emerging around 3,000-4,000 years ago within East Africa from a cowpox-like ancestor. Based on detailed studies of ancient DNA it seems that subsequently, the VARV genome continued to mutate and two distinct types (clades) have been identified within archaeological sources. One clade – termed modern VARV (mVARV) – has, so far, been traced back to the seventeenth century whereas another clade – termed ancient VARV (aVARV) – has been identified in burials from the seventh to eleventh century. The terminology being used is, in my view, a little misleading as it is important to appreciate that aVARV and mVARC are actually sister clades with a common genetic ancestor. The point at which mVARC and aVARC diverged from each other is critical in determining if it is possible for the Antonine Plague to have been caused by our modern variola virus (mVARC). Two recent studies suggest that this divergence probably happened during the Roman era, either between 200BC and 600 or between 160 and 500. Such data is helpful but, with the wide date ranges, far from conclusive in equating the modern-day smallpox virus with the organism that caused the Antonine Plague.

One other helpful piece of evidence is the discovery of a case of osteomyelitis variolosa in Roman skeletal remains from Cirencester dated to around the third or fourth century. This rare condition, due to smallpox, causes irreparable bone or joint damage in around 0.5 per cent of infected children. Importantly, the skeletal abnormalities persist into adulthood and can sometimes be identified in archaeological finds. Intriguingly, twenty years ago, the remains of at least ninety-one hurriedly buried individuals were also uncovered in a mass grave in nearby Gloucester. The pit contained a tangle of skeletal parts, so contorted and intermeshed as to imply that all the bodies had been tipped in at thc same time. Although it is impossible to prove that the individuals died due to the Antonine Plague, the dating evidence from the grave is in-keeping with burial at around that time. Moreover, alternative explanations for a mass grave of this type – warfare or famine – are not consistent with the osteological findings. Nearly half of the individuals were young adults with no signs of malnutrition, injuries, or chronic illnesses.

Based on the reported impacts (i.e. the likely infectivity and case-fatality), the genetics, and the paleopathology it is possible that the Antonine Plague is synonymous with smallpox. It also seems that, in common with smallpox, outbreaks of the Antonine Plague were generally associated with colder weather. However, a characteristic feature of smallpox is its strict specificity for humans and yet both Herodian and Aelius Aristides commented that the Antonine Plague affected animals too. Also, returning to Galen's various comments on the clinical features of the Antonine Plague, it difficult to understand why there was no specific mention of any of the common sequalae of smallpox such as pockmarks and scarring (especially on the face). In contrast, he highlighted some of the less typical symptoms of smallpox such as bowel problems, catarrh and coughing. But it is worth bearing in mind that scarring, bowel problems, catarrh and coughing vary between the different orthopoxvirus species too. For example, catarrh and coughing occur more often in monkey pox than smallpox and, although both species can cause scarring, the damage produced by smallpox is much worse and more disfiguring.

My overall conclusion is that the Antonine Plague was probably caused by a type of orthopoxvirus that was both lethal and highly transmissible, but the current evidence is insufficient to suggest any greater precision about the species.

Diagnostic Conjectures and Historical Understanding

Illness

The sections on Marcus Aurelius and Lucius Verus in the *SHA* both reported a single episode of sickness affecting Lucius: 'when he set out for the Parthian War, Marcus accompanied him to Capua; from there on he gorged himself in everyone's villas, fell sick and was ill at Canusium'. A surviving letter from Fronto to Lucius Verus, probably relating to the same episode of illness, provided some additional information:

> But on receipt of your letter, the very fact that you had written with your own hand raised my hopes at the outset; then came your good news that after three days' fasting and a prompt and rather drastic letting of blood you had been freed from the risk of a threatened illness.

Given the coverage and Fronto's obvious concerns it is suggested that this was an important illness. Lucius was also subjected to significant medical interventions incorporating three days of fasting and the removal of a considerable amount of blood. The physician Galen had advocated the use of phlebotomy (combined with moderation in food and drink) in 'patients liable to be seized with diseases…such as epilepsy, apoplexy, scotomatic diseases, haemoptysis and melancholy'. But Galen also commented that 'when I first came to Rome I found certain physicians who avoided phlebotomy so sedulously that even when a person was suffering from plethora they refused to use the remedy'. Perhaps the use of such an extreme regimen by the imperial physicians around 162 (and shortly prior to Galen's arrival in Italy) underlines the seriousness of Lucius Verus' condition.

Death

In 168, to counter the aggression from the Marcomannic confederation, Marcus Aurelius and Lucius Verus relocated their military headquarters to Aquileia. But the following year, and because of the Antonine Plague, a decision was made to return to Rome. Lucius Verus died en route at the town of Altinium.

This unexpected death in 169 has been ascribed to the Antonine Plague and on many occasions he would certainly have been in close proximity to those suffering from the disease. But the two detailed reports of the events surrounding Lucius Verus' death within the *SHA* are inconsistent with such a suggestion:

> Clad in the military cloak the two emperors finally set forth… advanced as far as Aquileia… Finally, they crossed the Alps, and pressing further on, completed all measures necessary for the defence of Italy and Illyricum. But on the way, after they had set out upon their journey, Lucius, sitting in the carriage with his brother, was seized with apoplexy and died [*sedens cum fratre in vehiculo Lucius apoplexi arreptus periit*].

> But, not far from Altinum, Lucius was struck down in the carriage with the sudden illness which they call apoplexy [*subito in vehiculo morbo, quem apoplexin vocant*]. After being set down from the carriage and bled, he was taken to Altinum, and after living on speechless for three days he died there.

Apoplexy is a broad term and Galen defined it as 'a paralysis of the whole body, together with impairment of its main functions'. Elsewhere, Galen indicated that it was characterised by a sudden onset, damage to the voice and, generally a fatal outcome. He also viewed it as being caused by an influx of blood into the brain or from the accumulation of phlegm and black bile within the cerebral ventricles. Immediate evacuation of blood by means of phlebotomy was the preferred treatment for apoplexy according to Galen.

Equating Lucius Verus' apoplexy with any specific modern equivalent is tricky. But, from the description provided by the *SHA* in the context of Galen's writings it does not seem unreasonable to suggest that Lucius Verus succumbed to some type of acute brain disorder such as an ischaemic stroke or a cerebral haemorrhage. It is also possible that Lucius Verus' purported lifestyle – in particular his diet and excessive alcohol consumption – might have increased his risk of suffering from a cerebral event. Lucius Verus' only previous episode of sickness reported by Fronto and treated by bloodletting and fasting is intriguing. Perhaps this earlier illness was linked to his eventual death in the same way that a transient ischaemic attack today is associated with a subsequent stroke.

In suggesting that an acute cerebral event was the cause of Lucius Verus' demise one difficulty is that he died relatively young at the age of 38. However, although the highest prevalence of strokes does certainly occur in adults after the age of 55, it can impact younger adults too associated with certain underlying conditions or risk factors. One specific issue that is particularly relevant in the case of Lucius Verus is his poor family health history with his father, Lucius Aelius Caesar also dying aged 36. According to Cassius Dio, 'Lucius Aelius Caesar was suddenly carried off by a severe haemorrhage' but the precise nature of the severe haemorrhage (αἵματος πολλοῦ) is difficult to ascertain. The *SHA* also stated that, following his adoption by Hadrian, he was too unwell to deliver an acceptance speech with Hadrian subsequently lamenting that 'We have leaned against a falling wall and we have lost the 300 million sesterces that we gave the people and the soldiers to mark the adoption'. However, it has been argued that Hadrian would have been extremely unlikely to have adopted an individual who was chronically unwell so, as in the case of his son Lucius Verus, it is suggested that Lucius Aelius' death was equally unexpected.

A final issue to be addressed in relation to the sudden death of Lucius Verus is whether there might have been any foul play. Cassius Dio wrote:

> Lucius gloried in these exploits and took great pride in them, yet his extreme good fortune did him no good; for he is said to

have engaged in a plot later against his father-in-law Marcus and to have perished by poison before he could carry out any of his plans.

According to the *SHA*, 'There is a well-known tale…that Marcus handed Verus part of a sow's womb smeared with poison after he had cut it with a knife poisoned on one side…we shall not leave it in the balance, but reject the whole story as disproved and refuted'. Although there were personal differences and occasional disagreements between the co-emperors it seems extremely unlikely that Marcus would have turned to poisoning his colleague. Marcus Aurelius accompanied Lucius' body back to Rome and, following the funeral ceremonies, Lucius was deified under the name of *Divus Verus*.

CHAPTER 12

Conclusion

Diagnosing the illnesses of Roman emperors might not be viewed as an appropriate line of enquiry given the enormous gulf that separates ancient and modern medicine. Physicians engaged in uncovering historical diseases have – somewhat disparagingly – been categorised as hobbyists simply dabbling in the medical past.

However, although there are certainly some major challenges in using present medical knowledge to identify past diseases, there are potential opportunities too in augmenting – or even correcting – the historical record.

By undertaking a detailed evaluation of the ancient sources relating to Augustus, he has been re-characterised as an individual surviving to the age of 75 with a long-term lung condition. Perhaps some of his enigmatic behaviours and actions represented a reaction to developing a chronic disease at a young age. As he began to come to terms with his predicament, some initial distress and anger were replaced by acceptance, adjustment and adaptation.

Claudius suffered from a movement disorder that affected his mobility and speech. He was also troubled by some uncontrolled movements and balance problems. Although Claudius was probably highly intelligent, the response of the Imperial family to his disability was to keep him in the shadows, out of politics and public affairs. He became of a figure of fun, ridiculed within Roman high society and subjected to insults and cruel tricks. The stresses, indignities and hardships that Claudius experienced in his youth and as a young man probably had an impact on his character, health and behaviour. Also, it seems much more likely that he died due to a stroke or a heart attack rather than from consuming poisoned mushrooms.

Marcus Aurelius might not have been as physically unwell as has been suggested by both modern and ancient historians. Despite suffering from sinus infections (with colds and sore throats), occasional gastroenteritis plus various aches and pains, there is no suggestion that he was troubled by any significant or chronic health problems. But it does seem likely that he had a dependence on opium-containing theriac, and he might have sought to end his own life.

In generating retrospective diagnoses of historical figures, issues such as context, definition, classification and language alongside ensuring a systematic approach to data collection and evaluation are frequently sidelined in favour of a much narrower focus on translations of historical reports detailing symptoms and signs. Although it does not seem unreasonable for modern physicians to draw on their clinical and scientific knowledge, this needs to be done cautiously and sparingly. Moreover, as a medical doctor, I simply could not have undertaken the work for this book without the fantastic support and guidance I have received from a range of other experts: classicists, linguists, historians, philosophers and archaeologists.

In relation to the process of diagnosis, I have argued that there are similarities between many of the issues I faced as a general practitioner (primary care physician) and those I have subsequently experienced as a retrospective diagnostician. In both circumstances I have encountered confusing or vague descriptions of possible clinical features alongside a requirement to rely on descriptive information. Also, primary care and retrospective diagnosticians must accommodate high levels of uncertainty. To ensure that any retrospective diagnostic outputs are contextualised, entirely based on the available data sources and at an appropriate level of precision, having the primary care model in mind can be invaluable.

Medical history has been particularly cruel to some historical figures. The, so-called, 'mad emperors' Caligula, Tiberius and Nero cannot question their various psychiatric diagnoses or request a second opinion. Neither can Nero or Caligula demand further testing to refute or confirm the suggestions that they both suffered from a type of hormonal disorder. The Hippocratic Oath serves to remind both ancient and modern doctors of the importance of doing no harm (*primum non nocere*). Perhaps we also need to keep this principle in mind when we are acting as retrospective diagnosticians by ensuring that our approach is both methodologically rigorous and multidisciplinary.

APPENDIX 1

Destillatio in the Writings of Celsus (tr, W.G. Spencer, 1935)

Celsus *De Medicina*	**Latin text**	**Translation**
1.2.3	…quae res maxime gravidines destillationesque concitat	…a thing which excites particularly choked nostrils and running colds
1.5.1	…aquae frigidae prodest, sed iis etiam, quos adsiduae lippitudines, gravidines, destillationes tonsillaeque male habent	…that find the use of cold water beneficial, but also those who suffer with persistent running of the eyes, choked nostrils and running from the nose, and tonsillar maladies
1.5.2	Vitari etiam gravidines destillationesque possunt, si quam minime qui his opportunus est loca aquasque mutet	Choked nostrils and running from the nose can be avoided, or minimised, if one who is liable to these makes as little change as possible in respect to residence and water
2.1.7	Vero… gravidines, destillationes	Spring…choked nostrils, runnings from the nose
2.1.14	Hiemps…Ceteros lippitudo arida et, si seniores sunt, gravedines atque destillationes male habent	Winter…Other people are attacked by dry ophthalmia, and if elderly by choked nostrils and runnings from the nose

Celsus *De Medicina*	**Latin text**	**Translation**
2.1.15	At si sicca aestas aquilones habuit, autumn vero imbres austrique sunt, tota hieme, quae provima est, tussis, destillatio, raucitas, in quibusdam etiam tabes oritor	If a summer has been kept dry by northerly winds, but in the autumn there are showers and south winds, there may then arise cough, runnings from the nose, hoarseness, and indeed in some, consumption
2.1.23	Praeter haec graciles tabes, deiectiones, destillationes, item viscerum et laterum dolores fatigant	In addition, thin people are fatigued by consumption, diarrhoea, running from the nose, pain in the lung and side
2.7.3	Frequens autem destillatio in corpore tenui longoque tabem timendam esse testatur	Again, running from the nose recurring often in a slender and tall man is a sign that consumption is to be apprehended
2.7.28	…post nimias destillationes tabes, post lateris dolorem vitia pulmonum	…consumption after excessive runnings from the nose; lung diseases after pain in the side
2.8.22	In pulmonis morbo… periculosa sunt tussis, destillatio, etiam quod alias salutare habetur, sternumentum	In pulmonary disease… the following are signs of danger: cough, catarrh, and even sneezing, which in other maladies is held salutary

Celsus *De Medicina*	**Latin text**	**Translation**
3.2.8-9	Quod si mali plus est et vera pthisis est… cavendae destillationes, ne, si quid cura levarit, exasperent	But if there is a more serious illness and a true consumption…he should be warned against catarrh, lest that should make worse what the treatment is relieving
4.5.1	Destillat autem de capite interdum in nares, quod leve est; interdum in fauces, quod peius est; interdum etiam in pulmonem, quod pessimum est. Si in nares destillavit, tenuis per has pituita profluit; caput leviter dolet, gravitas eius sentitur, frequentia sternumenta sunt; si in fauces, has exasperat, tussiculam movet; si in pulmonem, praeter sternumenta et tussim est etiam capitis gravitas, lassitudo, sitis, aestus, biliosa urina	Again, there is dripping from the head sometimes into the nose, which is a mild affair; sometimes into the throat, which is worse, sometimes into the lung, which is worst of all. When the drip is into the nostrils, a thin phlegm is discharged from them; there is slight pain, and a feeling of weight in the head, with frequent sneezing; if the drip is into the throat, it irritates and excites a slight cough; if the drip is into the lung, besides the sneezing, cough and even weight in the head, there is lassitude, thirst, a feeling of heat, and bilious urine

Celsus *De Medicina*	**Latin text**	**Translation**
4.5.2-4	…nunc video apud Graecos in gravedine hoc nomen servari, destillationem κατασταγμόν appellari. Haec autem et brevia et, si neglecta sunt, longa esse consuerunt. Nihil pestiferum est, nisi quod pulmonem exulceravit…	...I note that now the Greeks reserve this term for gravedo, the dripping they call catastagmus. These affections are commonly of short duration, but if neglected may last a long while. None is fatal, except that which causes ulcers in the lung…
	Quo levato, si in destillatione crassa facta pituita est, vel in gravedine nares magis patent, balineo utendum est, multaque aqua prius calida, post egelida fovendum os caputque; deinde cum cibo pleniore vinum bibendum	When the disease has been relieved so that the drip of phlegm becomes thick, or the gravedo so that the nostrils are more open, the bath may be resumed, much water, at first hot, then lukewarm, being used to foment the face and head; next, along with more food, wine may be taken

APPENDIX 2

Titles and Translations of Greek and Roman Literary Sources

Author & Title	**English Title**	**Edition(s) & Translation(s)**
Aelius Aristides *Orationes*	*Orations*	Behr (1981 & 1986)
Appian *Bella civilia*	*The Civil Wars*	Carter (1996)
Appian	*Illyrian Wars*	White (2024)
Cassius Dio *Historia Romana*	*Roman History*	Foster (1914) Scott- Kilvert (1987) [Augustus]
Celsus *De medicina*	*On Medicine*	Spencer (1935)
Columella *De re rustica*	*On Agriculture*	Ash (1941)
Dioscorides *De materia medica*	*On Medical Material*	Beck (2005)
Frontinus *Strategemata*	*Stratagems*	Bennett (1925)
Fronto *Epistulae ad M. Caes.; De Nepote Amisso; Ad Verum Imp.*	*Letters to Marcus Aurelius, Lucius Verus and Others*	Haines (1919)
Galen *De antidotis*	*Antidotes*	Kühn (1833) [14.1-209K]
Galen *Ars medica*	*The Art of Medicine*	Johnston (2016)

Author & Title	**English Title**	**Edition(s) & Translation(s)**
Galen *De atra bile*	*Black Bile*	Grant (2000)
Galen *De constitutione artis medicae*	*The Constitution of the Art of Medicine*	Johnston (2016)
Galen *De causis morborum*	*Causes of Diseases*	Johnston (2006)
Galen *De causis symptomatum*	*Causes of Symptoms*	Johnston (2006)
Galen *De curandi ratione per venae sectionem*	*Treatment by Bleeding*	Brain (1986)
Galen *De libris propriis*	*My Own Books*	Singer (1997)
Galen *De locis affectis*	*Affected Parts*	Siegel (1976)
Galen *De methodo medendi*	*The Method of Medicine*	Johnston and Horsley (2011)
Galen *Quod optimus medicus sit quoque philosophus*	*The Best Doctor is also a Philosopher*	Singer (1997)
Galen *De parvae pilae exercitio*	*On Exercise with the Small Ball*	Johnston (2018)
Galen *De praecognitione* [*ad Epigenem*]	*On Prognosis* [*for Epigenes*]	Nutton (1979)
Galen *De sanitate tuenda*	*On Hygiene*	Johnston (2018)
Galen *De symptomatum differentiis*	*The Distinct Types of Symptom*	Johnston (2006)

Author & Title	**English Title**	**Edition(s) & Translation(s)**
Galen *De temperamentis*	*Mixtures*	Singer (1997)
Galen *De theriaca ad Pisonem*	*On Theriac, for Piso*	Leigh (2016)
Galen *Thrasybulus sive Utrum medicinae sit aut gymnasticae hygiene*	*Thrasybulus, Whether Hygiene Belongs to Medicine or Physical Training*	Johnston (2018)
Galen *De tranquillitate animi*	*Avoiding Distress*	Singer (2013)
Galen *De tumoribus praeter naturam*	*Unnatural Swellings*	Lytton and Resuhr (1978)
Galen *De usu partium*	*The Use of Parts of the Body*	May (1968)
Galen *De venae sectione adversus Erasistrateos Romae degentes*	*Bloodletting, Against to Erasistrateans in Rome*	Brain (1986)
Gellius *Noctes Atticae*	*Attic Nights*	Rolfe (1927)
Herodian	*History of the Empire*	Whittaker (1969)
Herodotas *Historiai*	*Histories*	Holland (2013)
Hippocrates	*Aphorisms* *Regimen in Health* *Humours* *Regimen I, II, III* *Dreams*	Jones (1923), Volume 4
Hippocrates	*Prognostic* *Regimen in Acute Diseases*	Jones (1923), Volume 2

Author & Title	**English Title**	**Edition(s) & Translation(s)**
Hippocrates	*Epidemics I and III* *The Oath* *Nutriment*	Jones (1923), Volume 1
Homer	*Iliad*	Fagles (1992)
Horace *Satirae*	*Satires*	Juster (2008) Kilpatrick (1986)
Josephus *Antiquitates Judaicae*	*Jewish Antiquities*	Thackeray (1926) Wiseman (2013) [Caligula]
Justinian *Digesta*	*The Digest*	Scott (1932)
Juvenal *Saturae*	*Satires*	Rudd (1992)
Lactantius *De mortibus persecutorum*	*On the Deaths of the Persecutors*	Dalrymple (2021)
Livy *Ab urbe condita*	*History of Rome*	Foster (1989)
Marcellus Empiricus *De medicamentis*	*On Medicines*	Helmreich (1889)
Marcus Aurelius	*Meditations*	Staniforth (1964) Haines (1916) Gill (2013)
Nicolaus Damascenus	*Life of Augustus*	Hall (1923) Bellemore (1984) Toher (2016)
Pausanias	*Description of Greece*	Jones (1918)
Philo *Legatio ad Gaium*	*The Embassy to Gaius*	Colson (1962)
Philostratus *Vita Apollonii*	*Life of Apollonius of Tyana*	Jones (2005)
Pliny *Epistulae*	*Letters*	Radice (1963)

Author & Title	**English Title**	**Edition(s) & Translation(s)**
Pliny *Naturalis historia*	*Natural History*	Jones (1956)
Plutarch *Moralia*	*Morals*	Babbit (1931)
Plutarch *Quaestiones convivales*	*Table-Talk*	Clement and Hoffleit (1969)
Plutarch *Vitae [Brutus; Sulla]*	*Plutarch's Lives*	Perrin (1918)
Quintillian *Institutio oratoria*	*Institutes of Oratory*	Butler (1920)
Scribonius Largus *Compositiones medicamentorum*	*The Composition of Remedies*	Bernhold (1786) [in Latin]
Seneca *Apocolocyntosis*	*The Pumpkinification of the Divine Claudius*	Eden (1984)
Seneca *De beneficiis*	*On Benefits*	Basore (1928/1935)
Seneca *Epistulae morales*	*Letters From a Stoic*	Campbell (2004)
Seneca *De ira*	*On Anger*	Basore (1928/1935)
Scriptores Historiae Augustae (*SHA*) [*Hadrian, Antoninus Pius, Marcus Aurelius, Lucius Verus, Maximinus*]	*Historia Augusta*	Birley (1976) Magie (1921)
Suetonius *De vita Caesarum* [Julius Caesar, Augustus, Tiberius, Caligula, Claudius, Nero, Vespasian, Titus]	*Lives of the Caesars*	Graves (1957) Rolfe (1997) Wardle (1994) [Caligula] Wardle (2014) [Augustus]

Author & Title	**English Title**	**Edition(s) & Translation(s)**
Suetonius *De poetis*	*Lives of Poets*	Rolfe (1997)
Tacitus *De vita Iulii Agricolae*	*The Agricola*	Mattingly and Handford (1970)
Tacitus *Annales*	*The Annals*	Grant (1973) Jackson (1937)
Tacitus *Historiae*	*The Histories*	Wellesley (1972)
Valerius Maximus	*Memorable Deeds*	Speed (1678)
Velleius Paterculus	*The Roman History*	Shipley (1924)
Varro *De re rustica*	*On Agriculture*	Hooper and Ash (1935)
Vitruvius *De architectura*	*On Architecture*	Granger (1998)

Bibliography

Translations of Ancient Sources

Ash, H.B., (1941). *Columella: On Agriculture (Loeb Classical Library).* Cambridge, MA: Harvard University Press.

Babbit, F.C., (1931). *Plutarch Moralia 3. Sayings of the Romans.* Harvard: Harvard University Press.

Basore, J.W., (1928/1935). *Seneca: Moral Essays (Loeb Classical Library).* Cambridge, MA: Harvard University Press.

Beck, L.Y., (2005). *De materia medica by Pedanius Dioscorides.* Hildesheim, Germany: Olms-Weidmann.

Behr, C.A., (1981 & 1986). *P. Aelius Aristides: The Complete Works.* Leiden: Brill.

Bellemore, J., (1984). *Nicolaus of Damascus: Life of Augustus.* Edited With Introduction, Translation and Commentary. Bristol: Bristol Classical Press.

Bennett, C.E., (1925). *Frontinus: Stratagems; Aqueducts of Rome (Loeb Classical Library).* Cambridge, MA: Harvard University Press.

Bernhold, J.M., (1786). *Scribonii Largi. Compositiones Medicamentorum.* Milton Keynes: Lightening Source.

Birley, A., (1976). *Lives of the Later Caesars.* Reading: Penguin Books.

Brain, P., (1986). *Galen on Bloodletting.* Cambridge: Cambridge University Press.

Butler, E., (1920). *Quintillian. Institutio Oratario. Translation.* Harvard: Harvard University Press.

Campbell, R., (2004). *Seneca: Letters from a Stoic.* London: Penguin.

Carter, J., (1996). *Appian. The Civil Wars.* Translated With an Introduction. London: Penguin.

Clement, P.A. and Hoffleit H.B., (1969). *Plutarch: Moralia*, Volume VIII: *Table-Talk*, Books 1-6 *(Loeb Classical Library)*. Cambridge, MA: Harvard University Press.

Colson, F.H., (1962). *Philo: The Embassy to Gaius*. Translation *(Loeb Classical Library)*. Cambridge, MA: Harvard University Press.

Dalrymple, D., (2021). *On the Deaths of the Persecutors: A Translation of De Mortibus Persecutorum by Lucius Caecilius Firmianus Lactantius*. New Jersey: Evolution Publishing.

Eden, P.T., (1984). *Seneca Apocolocyntosis*. Cambridge: Cambridge University Press.

Fagles, R., (1992). *The Iliad*. London: Penguin Classics.

Foster, B.O., (1989). *Livy: History of Rome (Loeb Classical Library)*. Cambridge, MA: Harvard University Press.

Foster, H.B., (1914). *Dio Cassius: Roman History (Loeb Classical Library)*. Cambridge, MA: Harvard University Press.

Gill, C., (2013). *Marcus Aurelius Meditations*. Books 1-6. Translated With an Introduction and Commentary. Oxford: Oxford University Press.

Granger, F., (1998). *Vitruvius: On Architecture (Loeb Classical Library)*. Cambridge, MA: Harvard University Press.

Grant, M., (1973). *Tacitus: The Annals of Imperial Rome*. London: Penguin.

Grant, M., (2000). *Galen on Food and Diet*. Abingdon: Routledge.

Graves, R., (1957). *Suetonius: The Twelve Caesars*. London: Penguin.

Hall, C.M., (1923). *Nicolaus of Damascus: Life of Augustus. A Historical Commentary Embodying a Translation*. G. Banta.

Haines, C.R., (1916). *Marcus Aurelius: Meditations*. Cambridge, Mass.: Harvard University Press.

Haines, C.R., (1919). *The Correspondence of Marcus Cornelius Fronto*. 2 Volumes. London: *(Loeb Classical Library)*. Cambridge, MA: Harvard University Press.

Helmreich, G., (1889). *Marcelli: De medicamentis*. Leipzig: Teubner.

Holl, K., Kloft, H., and Fesser, (2001). *Caligula – Wilhelm II: Und der Cäsarenwahnsinn.* Bremen: Temmen.

Holland, T., (2013). *The Histories. Herodotus*. New York: Penguin.

Hooper, W.D. and Ash, H.B., (1935). *Cato and Varro on Agriculture (Loeb Classical Library)*. Cambridge, MA: Harvard University Press.

Jackson, J., (1937). *Tacitus: Annals.* London & Harvard: (Loeb Classical Library). Cambridge, MA: Harvard University Press.

Johnson, I., (2006). *Galen: On Diseases and Symptoms.* Cambridge: Cambridge University Press.

Johnson, I., and Horsley, G.H.R., (2011). *Galen: Method of Medicine (Loeb Classical Library).* Cambridge, MA: Harvard University Press.

Johnson, I., (2016). *Galen: On the Constitution of the Art of Medicine; The Art of Medicine; A Method of Medicine to Glaucon (Loeb Classical Library).* Cambridge, MA: Harvard University Press.

Johnson, I., (2018). *Galen: Hygiene; Thrasybulus; On Exercise With a Small Ball (Loeb Classical Library).* Cambridge, MA: Harvard University Press.

Jones, W.H.S., (1918). *Pausanias: Description of Greece (Loeb Classical Library).* Cambridge, MA: Harvard University Press.

Jones, W.H.S., (1923). *Hippocrates:* Volumes 1-8 *(Loeb Classical Library).* Cambridge, MA: Harvard University Press.

Jones, W.H.S., (1956). *Pliny: Natural History;* Volumes 1-10 *(Loeb Classical Library).* Cambridge, MA: Harvard University Press.

Jones, C.P., (2005). Philostratus. *Apollonius of Tyana,* Volume I: *Life of Apollonius of Tyana*, Books 1-4. (*Loeb Classical Library).* Cambridge, MA: Harvard University Press.

Juster, A.M., (2008). *The Satires of Horace.* Philadelphia, PA: University of Pennsylvania Press, 2008.

Kilpatrick, R.S., (1986). *The Poetry of Friendship. Horace, Epistles 1.* Alberta: University of Alberta Press.

Kühn, K.G., (1821-1833). *Claudii Galeni Opera Omnia.* Leipzig: C. Knobloch.

Leigh, R.A., (2016). *On Theriac to Piso, Attributed to Galen*. A Critical Edition with Translation and Commentary. Leiden: Brill.

Magie, D., (1921). *The Historia Augusta*. London & Harvard: (*Loeb Classical Library*). Cambridge, MA: Harvard University Press.

Mattingly, H. and Handford, S.A., (1970). *Tacitus: The Agricola and the Germania*. London: Penguin.

May, M.T., (1968). *Galen and the Usefulness of the Parts of the Body*. Translated from the Greek with an Introduction and Commentary. New York: Cornell University Press.

Nutton, V., (1979). *Galen: On Prognosis (De Praecognitione)*. Berlin: Akademie-Verlag.

Perrin, B., (1918). *Plutarch's Lives. An English Translation*. London: William Heinemann Ltd.

Radice, B., (1963). *The Letters of the Younger Pliny*. London: Penguin.

Rolfe, J.C., (1927). *The Attic Nights of Aulus Gellius*. London & Harvard: (*Loeb Classical Library*). Cambridge, MA: Harvard University Press.

Rolfe, J.C., (1997). *Suetonius* (2 volumes). London & Harvard: (*Loeb Classical Library*). Cambridge, MA: Harvard University Press.

Rudd, N., (1992). *Juvenal. The Satires*. Oxford: Oxford University Press.

Scott, S.P., (1932). *The Civil Law*. Cincinnati: The Central Trust Company.

Scott-Kilvert, I., (1987). *Cassius Dio – The Roman History: The Reign of Augustus*. London: Penguin Classics.

Shipley, F.W., (1924). *Velleius Paterculus: The Roman History*. Harvard: Harvard University Press.

Siegel, R.E., (1976). *Galen on the Affected Parts*. Translation from the Greek. Text with Explanatory Notes. New York: S. Karger.

Singer, P.N., (1997). *Galen: Selected Works*. Oxford: Oxford University Press.

Singer, P.N. (ed.). (2013). *Galen. Psychological Writings*. Cambridge: Cambridge University Press.

Speed, S., (1678). *Valerius Maximus: Memorable Deeds and Sayings*. Translation.

Spencer, W.G., (1935). *Celsus: De Medicina* (*Loeb Classical Library*). Cambridge, MA: Harvard University Press.

Staniforth, M., (1964). *Marcus Aurelius: Meditations*. Translated With an Introduction. Harmondsworth: Penguin Classics.

Thackeray, H.St.J., (1926). *Josephus: Jewish Antiquities*. A Translation. London. William Heinemann Ltd.

Toher, M., (2016). *Nicolaus of Damascus: The Life of Augustus and The Autobiography*. Edited With Introduction, Translations and Historical Commentary. Cambridge: Cambridge University Press.

Wardle, D., (1994). *Suetonius' Life of Caligula: A commentary*. Brussels: Latomus.

Wardle, D., (2014). *Suetonius. Life of Augustus (Vita Divi Augusti). Translated With Introduction and Historical Commentary*. Oxford: Oxford University Press.

Wellesley, K., (1972). *Tacitus: The Histories*. London: Penguin.

White, H., (2024). *Appian of Alexandria: The Foreign Wars*. UK: Independent.

Whittaker, C.R., (1969). *Herodian: History of the Empire*, Volume I: Books 1-4. Cambridge, MA: Harvard University Press.

Wiseman, T.P., (2013). *The Death of Caligula. Josephus Ant. Iud. XIX 1-273*, translation and commentary. Liverpool: Liverpool University Press.

Further Reading

Barrett, Anthony, (2002). *Livia: First Lady of Imperial Rome*. New Haven: Yale University Press.

Barrett, Anthony, (2015). *Caligula: The Abuse of Power*. London: Routledge.

Birley, Anthony, (1966). *Marcus Aurelius*. London: Eyre & Spottiswoode.

Cunningham, Andrew, (2016). *The Identity of the History of Science and Medicine*. Abingdon: Routledge.

Drinkwater, John, (2019). *Nero: Emperor and Court.* Cambridge: Cambridge University Press.

Eck, Werner, (2007). *The Age of Augustus.* Oxford: Blackwell.

Elliott, Colin, (2024). *Pox Romana: The Plague that Shook the Roman World.* Princeton: Princeton University Press.

Esser, Albert, (1958). *Cäsar und die Jusisch-Claudischen Kaiser im Biologisch-Ärtlichen Blickfeld.* Leiden: Brill.

Everitt, Anthony, (2006). *Augustus: The Life of Rome's First Emperor.* New York: Random House.

Goldsworthy, Adrian, (2014). *Augustus: First Emperor of Rome*. New Haven: Yale University Press.

Grmek, Mirko, (1989). *Diseases in the Ancient Greek World.* London: John Hopkins University Press Ltd.

Levick, Barbara, (1990). *Claudius.* London: Batsford.

Lewis, C.T. and Short, C., (2020). *A Latin Dictionary.* Chapel-en-le-Frith: Nigel Gourlay.

Liddell, H.G. and Scott, R., (1996). *A Greek-English Lexicon: With a Revised Supplement*. Oxford: Clarendon Press.

Nutton, Vivian, (2023). *Ancient Medicine.* London: Routledge.

Robertson, Donald, (2019). *How to Think Like a Roman Emperor. The Stoic Philosophy of Marcus Aurelius*. New York: St. Martin's Press.

Seager, Robin, (2005). *Tiberius.* Oxford: Blackwell.

Shotter, David, (1997). *Nero.* London: Routledge.

Notes

1. Foxhall, K. (2014). Making modern migraine medieval: men of science, Hildegard of Bingen and the life of a retrospective diagnosis. *Med Hist.* 58: pp. 354–374.
2. Sacks, O. (1995). *Migraine.* Basingstoke: Pan Macmillan. pp. 299–301.
3. Karenberg, A. (2009). Retrospective diagnosis: use and abuse in medical historiography. *Prague Med Rep.* 110: pp. 140–145.
4. Lorch, M. (2006). Language and memory disorders in the case of Jonathan Swift: considerations on retrospective diagnosis. *Brain* 129: pp. 3127–3137.
5. Rosenberg, C.E. (1992). Framing Disease: Illness, Society, and History, in Rosenberg, C.E. and Golden, J. (eds.). *Framing Disease: Studies in Cultural History.* New Brunswick: Rutgers University Press. pp. xiii–xxvi.
6. Leven, K.H. (2004). 'At times these ancient facts seem to lie before me like a patient on a hospital bed' – Retrospective diagnosis and ancient medical history, in Horstmanshoff, H.F.J. and Stol, M. (eds.). *Magic and Rationality in Ancient Near Eastern and Graeco-Roman Medicine*. Leiden: Brill, pp. 369–386.
7. Muramoto, O. (2014). Retrospective diagnosis of a famous historical figure: ontological, epistemic, and ethical considerations. *Philos Ethics Humanit Med.* 9: 10. doi:10.1186/1747-5341-9-10.
8. Scheidel, W. (1999). Emperors, Aristocrats, and the Grim Reaper: Towards a Demographic Profile of the Roman Elite. *The Classical Quarterly* 49: pp. 254–281.
9. Wardle, David (2023). E-mail to Nick Summerton dated 8 June 2023.
10. Suetonius, *Divus Augustus* 81.

11. Langslow, David (2023). E-mail to Nick Summerton dated 31 May 2023.
12. Crook, J. (1996). Augustus: Power, authority, achievement. In Bowman, A., Champlin, E. and Lintott, A. (eds.), *The Cambridge Ancient History* (The Cambridge Ancient History, pp. 113–146). Cambridge: Cambridge University Press. p. 77.
13. Nutton, Vivian (2023). E-mail to Nick Summerton dated 29 May 2023.
14. Badian, E. (1982). 'Crisis Theories' and the Beginning of the Principate. In: Wirth, G. (ed.) *Romanitas - Christianitas: Untersuchungen zur Geschichte und Literatur der römischen Kaiserzeit. Johannes Straub zum 70. Geburtstag am 18. Oktober 1982 gewidmet*. Berlin, Boston: De Gruyter. p. 31.
15. Wardle, D. (2007). A Perfect Send-off: Suetonius and the Dying Art of Augustus (Suetonius, Aug. 99). *Mnemosyne* 60: p. 443.
16. Wardle, D. (2008). Further thoughts on the death of Augustus. *Acta Classica* 51: p. 191.
17. Charlesworth, M.P. (1923). Tiberius and the Death of Augustus. *The American Journal of Philology* 44; p. 150.
18. Scarborough, J. (1975). The Drug Lore of Asclepiades of Bithynia. *Pharmacy in History* 17: p. 46.
19. Braudel, F. (1992). *The Structures of Everyday Life. Civilization and Capitalism 15th - 18th Century*. London: Fontana. p.310.
20. Crook, J. (1996). Augustus: Power, authority, achievement. In Bowman, A., Champlin, E. and Lintott, A. (eds.), *The Cambridge Ancient History* (The Cambridge Ancient History, pp. 113–146). Cambridge: Cambridge University Press. p. 78.
21. Wardle, D. (1994). *Suetonius' Life of Caligula: A commentary*. Brussels: Latomus. p. 155.
22. Katz, R.S. (1972). The Illness of Caligula. *The Classical World* 65: pp. 223–225; Katz, R.S. (1977). Caligula's Illness Again. *The Classical World* 70: pp. 451; Morgan, M.G. (1973). Caligula's Illness Again. *The Classical World* 66: pp. 327–329; Morgan, M.G.

(1977). Once Again Caligula's Illness. *The Classical World* 70: pp. 452–453.
23. Quidde, L. (1894). *Caligula: Eine Studie über römischen Cäsarenwahnsinn*. Leipzig: Friedrich; Freis, D. (2018). Diagnosing the Kaiser: Psychiatry, Wilhelm II and the Question of German War Guilt The William Bynum Prize Essay 2016. *Medical History* 62: pp. 273–294.
24. Sittig, F. (2018). *Psychopathen in Purpur: Julisch-Claudischer Caesarenwahnsinn Und Die Konstruktion Historischer Realitat: 249 (Historia - Einzelschriften)*. Stuttgart: Franz Steiner Verlag.
25. Barrett, A.A. (2015). *Caligula: The Abuse of Power.* London: Routledge, p. 258.
26. All parts of a yew tree are toxic to humans if swallowed so it is unclear exactly what is meant. Interestingly, the cancer chemotherapeutic drug *docetaxel*, that affects cell division, is derived from the European Yew. But, to date no formulation has been developed for skin application, unlike some other chemotherapeutic agents.
27. Horstmanshoff, M. (1999). Ancient medicine between hope and fear: medicament, magic and poison in the Roman Empire'. *European Review* 7: pp. 37–51.
28. Hooff, A.J.L. (1990). *From Autothanasia to Suicide: Self-killing in Classical Antiquity.* Abingdon: Routledge.
29. The dialogue between Marcus Aurelius and Fronto concerning illnesses (in over eighty of the extant letters) needs to be seen in the context of a second-century society noted for its interest in communicating about personal health problems and bodily ailments.
30. The term 'pituitosus' can also be translated as 'phlegm' and the adjective 'mucculentior' can be equated with our 'snivelling from the nose'.
31. Langslow, David. E-mail to Nick Summerton dated 15 November 2023. 'This letter – despite some possible corruption of the text – has been interpreted as indicating that Marcus Aurelius had a gastric ulcer but the word 'ulcus' can also be translated as 'a sore'.

Given the context, 'sore' seems a much more likely interpretation of 'ulcus'.

32. Freisenbruch, A. (2007). Back to Fronto: Doctor and Patient in His Correspondence with an Emperor. In *Ancient Letters: Classical and Late Antique Epistolography.* Edited by R. Morello and A.D. Morrison, 235–256. Oxford: Oxford University Press, p. 237.
33. Ibid., p. 248.
34. Dailly, R. and Van Effenterre, H. (1954). Le cas Marc-Aurèle. Essai de psychosomatique historique. *Revue des Études Anciennes* 56: pp. 347–365. The suggestion of a gastric ulcer was based on a combination of Cassius Dio's general comment supplemented by Fronto. In the mid-twentieth century, when Dailly and Van Effenterre were writing, there was a view that some physical diseases were linked to particular personality types or psychological profiles. Followers of the Paris Psychosomatic School in particular argued that there was a unity of the body and mind. But see note 31.
35. Hadot, P. (1995). *Philosophy as a Way of Life. Spiritual Exercises from Socrates to Foucault.* Oxford: Blackwell. p. 186.
36. Gill, C. (2013). *Marcus Aurelius Meditations*. Books 1–6. Translated With an Introduction and Commentary. Oxford: Oxford University Press, p. 38.
37. Van Ackeren, M. (2012). *A Companion to Marcus Aurelius.* Oxford: Blackwell.
38. Retief, F.P. (2007). Marcus Aurelius: was he an opium addict? *Acta Classica* 2: pp. 132–137; Africa, T.W. (1961). The opium addiction of Marcus Aurelius. *Journal of the History of Ideas* 22: pp. 97–102.

Index